LETTERS FROM THE ALMONER

NATHAN KRUPA

LETTERS FROM THE ALMONER

HOW AND WHY TO RAISE MONEY IN CHURCH

Copyright © 2018 by The Almoner.

All rights reserved. No part of this publication may be reproduced, distributed, or transmitted in any form or by any means, including photocopying, recording, or other electronic or mechanical methods, without the prior written permission of the publisher, except in the case of brief quotations embodied in critical reviews and certain other non-commercial uses permitted by copyright law. For permission requests, write to the publisher, addressed "Attention: Permissions Coordinator," at the address below.

The Almoner
P. O. Box 6805
Augusta, GA 30916–6805
thealmoner.com

Ordering Information:
Orders by U.S. trade bookstores and wholesalers.
Please contact Ingram Content at www.ingramcontent.com

Available in E-Book.

First Printing, 2018.

ISBN-13: 978-1-7327487-0-5

10 9 8 7 6 5 4 3 2 1

The Almoner™ and the associated logo are Trademarks of The Almoner.

Book Design by Catholic Way Publishing.

DEDICATION

To Father Mark. A good shepherd who taught me that feeding the sheep is more important than fleecing them.

THANKSGIVING

MANY THANKS TO ALL the people in my life who supported me in writing this book. First and foremost, I give thanks to God for the call to raise money to feed the hungry, and to Mike Firmin and Golden Harvest Food Bank for helping me to answer that call. Thanks to my supportive wife and family, who patiently endured the creative process. Thanks to Brice Sokolowski and CatholicFundraiser.net for inviting me to write the articles that became the seed for The Almoner.com and the opening chapters of this book. Special thanks to Mary Vizzini for her work editing the book and Peter Vizzini for contributing the beautiful book cover and the Almoner logo. The finished project would be inconceivable without them … inconceivable! Special thanks to Bishop Joel Konzen of the Archdiocese of Atlanta for his encouragement and support.

Contents

	Dedication	i
	Thanksgiving	i
	Preface	ix
1	Welcome to St. Catherine's!	1
2	Consider how Jesus fundraised!	5
3	Fundraise like a Franciscan	9
4	For everything there is a season … even in fundraising	13
5	Tax collecting vs. evangelizing	17
6	The WORST capital campaign in history!	21
7	Planning with God in mind	27
8	Opening the Eyes of the blind	31
9	Knock! knock! Who's there? Ben Hur!	37
10	Major gifts for beginners—Part One	43
11	Major gifts for beginners—Part Two	47
12	Major gifts for beginners—The Grand Finale!	51
13	The Rich Man and Lazarus— A Paradigm for Fundraising	55
14	Time, Talent, and the Fish with a Golden Tooth	61
15	No bake fundraising	67
16	Donations, and eyeballs, online	71
17	Grant expectations—Multiplication of the Gifts	75
18	Thou shalt see thy donor face to face!	79
19	Endowments—The fundraiser's apple seed	83
20	Asking for more than loose change	87
21	Time, talent, tithe = a life of prayer, service, and thanksgiving	91

22	Go therefore and make … stewards? No! Disciples!	97
23	Build an army of volunteer fundraisers	101
24	Entitlements are charity without Charity	105
25	Fundraising two by two, a biblical buddy system	109
26	Hurricanes—A time for talents	113
27	Casting a broader net; requests for support	117
28	The widow's might; the power of giving	121
29	Why stewardship? A personal testimony	127
30	Let's go fishing—acquiring new donors	131
31	Stocked up—a path to bigger gifts	135
32	Take arms against a sea of Mammon	137
33	Conversions for the web and the soul	145
34	Crying out for mercy	149
35	Be a grateful leper	151
36	Stewardship is only 10% about Church	155
37	Who are YOUR disciples?	161
38	Invest in Alabaster Jars	165
39	Our bucket is leaking!	169
40	Not a Drill, a planned emergency	173
41	Endowments—Tending the Orchard	177
42	A Christmas farewell	181
	Index	185

PREFACE

PEOPLE PUT FUNDRAISING right up there with wrestling alligators. It's great when you can watch someone else, but don't ask ME to do it! That's not the right way to think about it. Fundraising makes all kinds of amazing things possible and doing it well can give you quite a thrill.

Since most books about fundraising are about as exciting as watching a toaster, I tried to do something a little different. You're about to read a series of fictional letters from a professional fundraiser, The Almoner, to his parish Priest, Father Zagloba. You'll learn how to raise more money but also why raising money can be an invitation to deeper conversion—for the fundraiser as well as the donor.

If you think that this sounds a little like the Screwtape Letters, you're exactly right. Honestly, using letters to teach has a much older and holier pedigree than C. S. Lewis. Just look at the Gospel of Luke, the Book of Acts, and the rest of the New Testament epistles. While there's no way I'll live up to those standards, it's always better to aim high. My goal is to point you to the Truth.

May God grant that any wisdom I share serve you, and my folly do you no harm.

1.
WELCOME TO ST. CATHERINE'S!

Dear Fr. Zagloba,

WELCOME TO ST. CATHERINE'S! I know that you are excited to take on your first big assignment as pastor of our church, and I think that you'll do a wonderful job. We're a humble parish, but we have lots of energy and gifts that are ready to be put to work.

After your first Parish Council Meeting, I wanted to write a word of encouragement. When we got to the topic of the budget and all the repairs that our buildings need, it did look a little grim. I could see the look in your eyes when you realized that we were going to need to raise money just to get the roof repaired. I think I detected a little bit of, "Father, please let this cup be taken away from me," hidden behind your smile.

I have been there. When the Lord called me to be a professional fundraiser, I had no experience and not the slightest desire to do fundraising. Here I am seven years later, and I've raised four million dollars to feed the hungry. Amazing! God knows what He's doing, and He has chosen you as the man for the job. I will assist you in any way that I can.

One way I think I can help is to try to condense my fundraising experience and research and give you a solid foundation on which to build. I saw the Summa sitting on your desk, so I think you'll enjoy a good logical breakdown of the art of asking for alms. St. Thomas, pray for us!

THE RELATIONSHIP BETWEEN STEWARDSHIP AND FUNDRAISING

Stewardship and fundraising are two different things. Stewardship looks at the question of how we manage our time, our abilities, and our finances in a way that conforms to the Gospel. Stewardship teaches us to ask ourselves, "What should *I* do with *my* money?" Or maybe more broadly, "What does God want me to do with my resources?"

Fundraising looks at an interpersonal question. Fundraising asks, "Will *you* give some of *your* money to *me* to do such and such awesome thing?" Can you see the difference?

Preaching on stewardship might help you with fundraising because it gets people thinking about those first questions. However, it is not necessarily fundraising, especially if you never get to the point where you're asking the second question of "Will you give me money for [this thing]?" Fundraising REQUIRES an asking. You're not just prompting philosophical reflection about what values motivate people, you're asking them to get out their wallets, take out some bills, and put them in the basket.

BE ENCOURAGED!

Fundraising can seem like a daunting task, but you have been supernaturally empowered to lead our parish. Think about the early Church. The Apostles were NOT professional fundraisers. They were fishermen and tax collectors.

The book of Acts records the fact that people were selling their land to give it to the Apostles to be stewarded by them.

Why? It's something to ponder. Pray about it.

You are a member of the same priesthood and share the same divine mission of making disciples of all the nations.

God will inspire you to lead the Pastoral Council to do what He has planned. When we focus on doing what God wants us to do, He makes the impossible happen. That's exciting! I mean "parting the Red Sea" exciting.

Please forgive me if my letters sometimes get a little long. I get so excited about learning and living our Faith that my pen often overflows. Let me know where you want me to start in our discussion of fundraising, and I'll dive in.

Blessings,
The Almoner

P. S. In the old days, an almoner held the office in the church that asked for money to support charitable work with the poor. The Pope still has an almoner. Now, you do too!

2.
CONSIDER HOW JESUS FUNDRAISED!

Dear Fr. Zagloba,

YES, I AM SERIOUS THAT I do not consider bake sales fundraisers: neither are pancake breakfasts, Christmas cards, or egg roll sales for that matter. I agree that the Pancake Breakfast is an Institution, and I know that I will be able to stop the moon before I stop the Knights of Columbus from doing it. People enjoy it, but it is not fundraising.

Why? This distinction between what is and is not fundraising is vital.

Bake sales and all other forms of sales are businesses. What is a business? You make a product and then sell it at a price higher than your cost. The difference between those two values is your profit. In the history of the Church, there are plenty of great examples of these kinds of "charitable enterprises."

I love Trappist beer. Beer is an excellent example of the charitable enterprise model. The monks pray and make beer. They sell the beer and use the money to support their monastery. Prayer elevates everything, including beer making, which is why Trappist beer is so delicious. Is this fundraising? No: It is beer selling.

FUNDRAISING HAS A DIFFERENT FOCUS

In fundraising, you are "selling" the mission, not a product. Last week, I was in a parking lot. Crowding the street exit were a group of 13-year-old boys, wearing football uniforms, carrying signs, and using their helmets to collect donations. They were raising money to pay for football camp. They weren't offering anything in return for a donation, except for the warm fuzzy feeling of helping them do something good.

The boys' activity is fundraising at the most basic level. They wanted people who drove by them to buy into their mission. Their "ask" was, "If you give us money, it will support a wholesome summer activity for a bunch of boys who would otherwise be out getting into trouble."

I bought into their message, and I handed the boys a few dollars.

All fundraising must include an "ask." The basic components of an "ask" are: a need, a solution, and an offer. The boys' "need" was for good wholesome physical activity to keep them out of trouble. Their "solution" was summer football camp. The "offer" was: "Help us pay the costs of the field, equipment, and staff for football camp so we can become outstanding citizens."

Now, their "ask" didn't go so far as saying all those things explicitly, but you can see how they were all present. Clearly communicating those three elements makes for great fundraising.

WHEN YOU HAVE THE PEARL OF GREAT PRICE, DON'T SELL DOUGHNUTS

A few days later, two ladies carrying boxes of doughnuts approached me in a different parking lot. One told me that she was selling doughnuts to raise money for her mission trip to Africa. I'm a fan of mission trips. I, however, politely declined.

Why? Apart from not being hungry for a sugar rush, I did not want to give my money to buy a doughnut. The ladies were selling doughnuts, not the mission trip. The request was, "Will you BUY these DOUGHNUTS, so I can go build an orphanage in Africa?" Do you see the difference between their approach and that of the boys? It's a fine line, but that is why selling things is not fundraising. When you engage in a charitable enterprise (or business), you focus your potential donor on the benefit they will receive from their purchase. Whatever you try to sell—beer, doughnuts, rosaries, or books—your potential donors are asking themselves, "Do I want this [product]?"

Fundraising, on the other hand, focuses the donor on the good they will accomplish by giving their money. Fundraisers help donors get excited about being a part of something greater than themselves. You tell stories about the ministries that the Church will perform; the new members of the Church that will receive the sacraments; the outreach to the poor that will feed the hungry; the people who walk in darkness who will see a great Light. Their generosity will help make these moments possible.

For the potential donors, the "ask" invites their participation in the greater work of the Church. This moment, therefore, is also an opportunity for conversion! The potential donor must choose between holding onto his/her money and giving it away for the sake of the Gospel. Fundraising, then, supports a big idea, a mission, the creation of something new, or a ministry opportunity. It's much bigger than buying a donut or a cold beer.

JESUS DID NOT SELL CHAIRS TO SUPPORT HIS MINISTRY

Jesus, as a carpenter, likely made the best chairs ever. He did not, however, support his ministry by selling furniture. Instead, Jesus relied on donors—women, in fact—who gave of their resources BECAUSE THEY BELIEVED IN HIS MISSION. When the fullness of time arrived, he set aside his tools and preached the Kingdom. When he called His disciples, they also left their businesses (fishing and tax collecting, etc.) to preach the Gospel of the Kingdom.

When a person awakens to the Kingdom of God, they respond the same way the Apostles did. When your fundraising focuses on your mission, on "Go therefore and make disciples of all the nations," people get excited. They WANT to give because they have caught hold of a vision greater than themselves. This supernatural reality, not some business transaction, should be the foundation of your fundraising.

Plus, you don't have to wash the dishes required to bake 182,000 brownies.

Blessings,
The Almoner

3.

FUNDRAISE LIKE A FRANCISCAN

Dear Fr. Zagloba,

PERHAPS YOU ARE RIGHT.

In some ways, fundraising does sound a lot like begging. I understand that you don't want to look a beggar. Who does? I didn't either. I think the humiliation people feel around "begging" is a key reason why most people prefer to sell things when fundraising rather than ask people directly for money. People feel more comfortable selling brownies than asking for directly for donations, because it doesn't make them feel like a beggar.

I'm going to say something that might sting a little. I can say it because I've felt the pain myself. If you don't like being a beggar, you may need to examine your heart. You might have a bit of pride that tells you, "begging is beneath you." Even more, you may believe that beggars are beneath you.

I HAVE SHOCKING NEWS FOR YOU: JESUS WANTS YOU TO BE A BEGGAR

Consider how Jesus rolled out the Kingdom of God. When Jesus sent out the disciples to proclaim the Kingdom, did he give them chariots of fire to carry them or hosts of angels to warm up the crowd?

No. Instead, Jesus said, "Don't take gold, or silver, or copper for your belts, no sack for the journey, or a second tunic, or sandals, or walking stick" (Matthew 10:9–10).

He told them to go as beggars, and it worked. In fact, it worked so well that the greatest military in human history tried for 300 years to crush this kingdom of beggars and finally decided to convert.

You will notice that this is not a one-off or an accident. As if Jesus wanted to prove that his method worked, 1,200 years later, the Holy Spirit led Saint Francis and Saint Dominic to build their religious orders on the same principles He gave to the first disciples.

Why does it work? "Though he was rich, Jesus made himself poor so that through his poverty we might become rich" (2 Corinthians 8:9). Jesus has given you, me and everyone else this example to follow.

SAVING SOULS—ONE ONION AT A TIME

I have a friend, Brother Vincent, who is currently a Franciscan Friar in New York City. He spent a couple of years in Central America working with one of their apostolates. One of his jobs was to go to the marketplace every day and ask for bread from the vendors.

Brother Vincent told me that he would walk down the row of vegetable stands, asking for food for the love of God. The farmer whose stall was at the end of the row would see him coming and would always find something to do so he wouldn't have to answer him.

The farmer continued to ignore him for several months. Each time Brother Vincent would greet the farmer and ask gently for a gift for the love of God, the man would keep his back to him.

Then one day, Brother Vincent called out to him and the man stood up, turned around, picked up an onion and tossed it over. For the next couple of months, the man continued to respond, giving Brother Vincent a single onion each time he saw him. He was still gruff, but now he was giving.

Then, some months later, the man finally smiled at Brother Vincent, reached down and gave him two onions. From that day forward, he responded very kindly to the brother's requests.

Brother Vincent's humble requests for food slowly but surely opened the door for that farmer to experience a real conversion. His humble and persistent response to the farmer's rejection slowly chipped away at the hardness of his heart until, finally, a new relationship was born.

RIDE THIS DONKEY RIGHT INTO THE KINGDOM

When Jesus entered Jerusalem in triumph, he rode a donkey. For us, that donkey symbolizes humility. Taking on the rags of a beggar, like Christ, will transform your ministry in ways that you can't possibly imagine.

Why? Because that donkey is supernatural.

Blessings,
The Almoner

4.

FOR EVERYTHING THERE IS A SEASON …
EVEN IN FUNDRAISING

Dear Fr. Zagloba,

SO, I CAME OUT to my truck this morning and found that I had a flat tire.

Bummer!

What does this have to do with fundraising? I'll tell you.

The other day, I read an article on the topic of fundraising. He explained how he increased his offertory by 30% without even asking.

It was the same feeling I had when I found my truck with a flat tire: dumbstruck. Here I am, telling you that fundraising REQUIRES asking, and here he is describing how he succeeded without doing so. I looked at the article with the same expression that I had as I looked at a flat tire.

Here's the gist of what he said. He slashed the budget to get rid of unnecessary spending. He invested in small but visible improvements around the Church. He spoke from the pulpit regularly about the good things that were happening and even took one Sunday to explain the Parish's financial position. Never once did he ask for more money, but the people responded by increasing their giving by a whopping 30%.

So, what is going on here? I thought about this article for a couple of days, trying to understand how Fr. Alan's success fits in with my knowledge of fundraising.

Then it hit me: he was closing the loop on his parish appeal.

CATHOLICS ARE NOT ATMS IN A PARISH APPEAL

So far, I've mostly written about the 'asking' part of fundraising. I focus on this because it's the hardest part to do correctly and the easiest part to do wrong, but asking is just the beginning. Great fundraising focuses on fostering relationships with your donors.

Don't treat your parishioners like a cash machine that you can withdraw money from at any time. They recognize that attitude and don't like it. Rather, you must consider 'closing the loop,' which means recognizing that there is a life cycle to every donation, especially when you are running a parish appeal.

This life cycle is:

1. ASK for the gift.

2. RECEIVE the gift.

3. THANK the donor for the gift. Gratitude is vital yet often missed in church fundraising. I don't simply mean once, for example after someone gives. Gratitude done correctly is frequently done.

4. DO what you said you were going to do. You go out and accomplish it. You also communicate to everyone, not just donors, what you are achieving.

5. CELEBRATE. It's always important to communicate what you have accomplished with your donors. Take the necessary time to stop and enjoy the fruits of everyone's labor.

6. REPEAT the cycle.

I think a lot of donors feel trapped in the first part of the life cycle—always being asked for money. Their donations then get sucked into a black hole, never to be seen again. No one ever thanks them properly. Instead, they get jolted by being asked again without the satisfaction of enjoying and celebrating what their gift accomplished.

Fr. Alan realized that his parish had gotten stuck in the first two stages of the giving life cycle, asking and receiving. His parishioners were feeling neglected because they weren't being thanked properly and nothing seemed to be changing for the better. So, he began with Step 4: Doing. He took control of the budget, fixed several small signs of neglect and communicated both his gratitude and what he'd been working on. He completed Steps 3 (Gratitude), 4 (Doing), and 5 (Celebration) in the life cycle of giving, and, thus, made his parishioners happy.

YOU CAN'T BREAK THE CYCLE

It's important to recognize that behind each donation is a person, a story, and hard-earned dollars. A donation is never just a monetary transaction. When you complete the life cycle of fundraising by communicating and celebrating the outcomes and successes, people get excited about giving again because they know that their gift has made an impact. They also begin to trust that another gift will do the same.

By focusing on the DOING of being a good steward, Fr. Alan enabled his parish to CELEBRATE in a church that was more attractive, better managed and better maintained. The visual cue of newly painted walls helped the parishioners see how their gifts made an impact. As a result, they were willing to increase their gifts because they wanted to see even more good things happen.

THERE'S AN ASK IN THE BASKET!

I do have to disagree slightly with Father on one minor point. It's not entirely true that he didn't ask. He might not have SAID anything about increasing donations, but during every Mass, there is an "ask." Even if nobody talks about it. After the homily, when the ushers pass the baskets through the pews, that is an "ask." It's a gentle one, but I know from my personal experience that I feel it, especially when my wallet is empty.

By being a good steward himself and sharing the fruits of good stewardship with his parish, Fr. Alan improved the success of the bASKet. A 30% increase is extraordinary. I celebrate his tremendous accomplishment and rejoice that his parish responded so well to his loving attention. When he completed the life cycle and allowed parishioners to celebrate successful stewardship, the fundraising cycle started afresh and brought in more money.

I think I have plucked this thorn out of my understanding of fundraising and offertories. Now, I'm off to get that nail out of my tire!

Blessings,
The Almoner

5.

TAX COLLECTING VS. EVANGELIZING

Dear Fr. Zagloba,

WE HAD A GREAT VACATION! Thanks for asking. Strangely enough, I had a conversation during the wedding reception that applies directly to your question of how to approach talking about money with the parish.

One of my wife's college friends works as a business manager of a parish. The annual Stewardship campaign and offertory is his responsibility. He made a comment that captured my attention, and I've been thinking about it ever since.

He was talking about St. Matthew. Jesus walked up to him and said, "Follow me." Matthew stood up and walked away from his tax tables to become an apostle, evangelist and martyr. My wife's friend said he could understand. He feels like the tax collector in his parish, and he hates it. He wishes he could get up, leave tax collecting behind, and go follow Jesus.

THE GOSPEL OF ST. MATTHEW—FROM TAX COLLECTOR TO EVANGELIST

Think about St. Matthew. He was that guy everybody hated because he took their money and gave it to the Romans. Everything changed when Jesus came on the scene. The tax collector became an evangelist. St. Matthew quite literally got up and left a table full of money behind. Why?

The daily Mass reading a couple of days ago describes Jesus telling his disciples, "And everyone who has given up houses or brothers or sisters or father or mother or children or lands for the sake of my name will receive a hundred times more and will inherit eternal life" (Matthew 19:29).

I think there is a nugget of purest gold in here. Under the old covenant, it was your DUTY to give a tenth of your income to support the Temple, priests and Levites. The tithe was a religious tax. Jesus does not come to abolish the law, but to fulfill it. God doesn't NEED our gifts … we NEED to give. It is good for us! The radical change the Gospel proposes is, "Sell all you have and give it to the poor and then you will have treasure in heaven" (Matthew 19:21).

We're not supposed to give money to the church because we owe money to God (although, that isn't a bad reason). No! When we give to the church and the poor, God gives us 100 times more in return! Talk about the best investment plan in the entire universe!!!

IF YOU SEE YOURSELF AS A TAX COLLECTOR, YOU WILL HATE FUNDRAISING

The tax collector says to a person, "You owe this much." For this reason, people HATE tax collectors. They hide when they see them coming. They pay small fortunes to hide their money so tax collectors can't find it. If you think of yourself as a tax collector, if you approach this as a religious tax, you will hate this part of your work, and the parishioners will hate it, too.

The message of an evangelist is different. Jesus said, "Give, and gifts will be given to you; a good measure, packed together, shaken down, and overflowing, will be poured into your lap. For the measure with which you measure will in return be measured out to you" (Luke 6:38).

Do you see the total transformation? When the evangelist gets this message across to his audience, they respond the way people did in the Book of Acts. Whoever had land sold it and gave it to the disciples! Can you imagine this happening today?

THE GOOD NEWS OF GOD'S GENEROSITY

In our materialistic age, one of the hardest things for most people to wrap their minds around is that God WANTS to be our provider. Jesus said,

> So, do not worry and say, "What are we to eat?" or "What are we to drink?" or "What are we to wear?" All these things the pagans seek. Your heavenly Father knows that you need them all. But seek first the kingdom [of God] and his righteousness, and all these things will be given you besides. (Matthew 6:31–33)

When we seek God's Kingdom and His righteousness, God will give them to us. As a bonus, He will give us EVERYTHING ELSE THAT WE NEED! What an amazing truth! Totally life changing!

But here is the sticking point. Do WE believe this, Father? If we don't, then no one will believe you when you preach it as a part of our stewardship campaign. If you're like me, you're probably in a place where you're saying, "I believe, help my unbelief."

BLESSED ARE YOU WHO ARE POOR, FOR YOURS IS THE KINGDOM

Something that amazes me here in Georgia is that many of our new priests are coming from Africa. It puzzled me until I asked a seminarian from Nigeria why this is so. He said that in Africa, many people are forced by circumstances and poverty to rely on God for their daily bread. And guess what!?!!?!?! He answers their prayers! Over and over again. They must trust God … and they discover that He is trustworthy. This very concrete experience of God's provision leads to lots of vocations to the priesthood.

In America, our material wealth is the source of our spiritual poverty. Empty churches and seminaries are the fruit of a culture that is selfish and self-reliant. Our hope is founded in our 401(K), not on the Rock of our Salvation.

As an evangelist, you can point them to a greater reliance on the God who saves. You can help them to understand that ONLY the fullness of God can fill their deep hunger and longing. Their many possessions can't do it. St. Paul perhaps put it best in his first letter to Timothy:

> Tell the rich in the present age not to be proud and not to rely on so uncertain a thing as wealth but rather on God, who richly provides us with all things for our enjoyment. Tell them to do good, to be rich in good works, to be generous, ready to share, thus accumulating as treasure a good foundation for the future, so as to win the life that is true life. (1 Timothy 6:17–19)

When we give to the Church and the poor, we aren't putting money into an investment account that adds two zeros to the end of every dollar. No, I'm not advocating for the Prosperity Gospel. Instead, what we're doing is taking a leap of faith … trusting that the God who made all things will respond generously to our generosity. In return, God gives us the spiritual riches of His eternal kingdom—peace, joy, contentment, fulfillment, love.

Talk about Good News!!!

Blessings,
The Almoner

6.

THE WORST CAPITAL CAMPAIGN IN HISTORY!

Dear Fr. Zagloba,

NO, I THOUGHT YOUR homily was great! It hit just the right tone for kicking off our stewardship campaign. I'm sorry to hear that someone disagreed with you so strongly on your understanding of almsgiving. I don't think what they said was either correct or kind.

You were not promoting the Prosperity Gospel. You weren't selling indulgences. You were pointing out the very clear statements that Jesus made about how good almsgiving is for the person who gives.

I do think that it's important to make clear the huge chasm of difference between the evil that is the sin of 'simony' and the spiritual and practical benefits of almsgiving.

YOU CAN'T BUY HOLINESS (OR HOLY THINGS FOR THAT MATTER)!

Simon Magus, who gives us the name for the sin of "simony," tried to buy the Holy Spirit from the apostles. He saw the works they were doing—most especially the laying on of hands to confer the Holy Spirit—and thought that it was some commodity that he could buy. St. Peter, in turn, rebuked him fiercely for attempting to buy the gift of God.

Simony suggests that holiness and the gifts of God are things that you can go pick up at Walmart. This idea is nonsense and has been suppressed and rejected since the earliest days of the Church.

The spiritual and temporal benefits of Almsgiving are a different matter. When we give alms to the Church or the poor, we are not buying holiness. We are doing something that is holy. We are participating in holiness. And in a very real sense, we are encountering holiness in the Person of Christ as embodied in the Church and the poor.

THE MOST DISASTROUS CAPITAL CAMPAIGN IN HISTORY

Modern Catholics have a real difficulty talking about how almsgiving is good for us. We got it mixed up with selling indulgences and threw out the baby with the bath water. Before going any further, I need to point out the root of this confusion.

I'm talking about Johann Tetzel, the poor fundraising friar who ended up provoking the wrath of Martin Luther. I don't think historians have ever looked at poor Johann's story with a fundraiser's eyes, but I think it sheds some light on the story. Imagine little Johann as he grows up with a burning desire to be a preacher. He embraces a life of evangelical poverty and study by joining the Dominican Order. In his mind, maybe he thinks that someday he will follow in the footsteps of the great founder St. Dominic, or the legendary St. Thomas or St. Vincent Ferrer.

Instead, they make him a fundraiser. "Go, therefore, and raise money to build St. Peter's Basilica." Not the mission he thought he signed up for. But, like an obedient Dominican, he takes up his cross and searches for the best possible reason for people to donate money. According to the practice of the time, he focuses on the spiritual benefits conferred by almsgiving through the traditional practice of indulgences, which apply to both the living and the dead.

The practice of soliciting offerings to the Church for suffering souls in Purgatory comes from 2 Maccabees 12:40–44. You might remember: Several soldiers die during battle and are found to be wearing amulets to a false god. Judas Maccabeus takes up an offering of 2,000 drachmas for expiatory sacrifices for the dead because he believes in the resurrection. This scriptural testimony was so powerfully in favor of Tetzel's position that Luther tossed out both books of Maccabees when he changed the Bible.

Well, Johann perhaps goes a bit overboard in his preaching. The famous quote attributed to him is, "As soon as gold in the casket rings, the rescued soul to heaven springs." Some Catholic historians like Nikolaus Paulus dispute that Fr. Johann was quite so callous in his approach to indulgences, but in any event Martin Luther throws down the gauntlet. The 95 Theses get nailed to a church door, starting a war of words that ends in schism and war, in fact.

So, a poorly planned capital campaign—BOOM!—ignites the Protestant Reformation. Fr. Johann tries to defend his preaching and Church teaching, suffers a nervous break-down over the whole affair, and dies in sorrow. Let this be a warning to us to do our homework before trying to start a capital campaign. Bad fundraising can have BAD consequences.

Now, I am not trying to pick a fight regarding the practices surrounding indulgences at that time. I know there were, in fact, real abuses. Some of the faithful did unfortunately view indulgences as a way of buying a ticket to heaven. Any student of history knows that. But the abuse, the misuse, the corruption of the real nature of almsgiving does not in any way abolish the very real good that comes from it.

LOVE IS GENEROUS!!!

The Prosperity Gospel treads very close to simony by saying, "Give your tithe to this church, and God will begin to pour out the blessings of wealth and material prosperity upon you." The nugget of truth in what they say is that God has in fact promised to bless our giving, but they focus on the gift, not the giver. You're not purchasing heavenly favor with your giving. God's gifts are not for sale. Your main focus can't be on the blessing that you want, as St. Paul points out: "If I give away everything I own, and if I hand my body over so that I may boast but do not have love, I gain nothing" (1 Corinthians 13:3). If love doesn't motivate the gift, if your focus is solely on what you're going to get because you give, then God won't give you ANYTHING!

Love is the key ... to pretty much everything. We give to the Church because we love Her. We give to the poor because we love them. Every gift that we give in the spirit of love pleases God, and He responds with the generosity that His infinite bounty makes possible. At the heart of the Gospel is the economy of the gift. God gives because He is Love. We give back because we have been loved and love in return.

ALMSGIVING IS NOT ONLY GOOD; IT IS GOOD FOR YOU!

Our gifts to the Church and the poor do not purchase a golden ticket to heaven. No, each gift is a thanksgiving offering to God who has already given us everything. And in the exchange of gifts, He always insists on having the First and the Last Word. First, He so loves us that He gives us His Word. And last, at the end of our mortal life, He gives back to us 100 times what we have given Him, plus eternal life. "And this is eternal life, that they know You and Jesus Christ whom You have sent" (John 17:3).

You see, God is the wealthy father who provides a lavish feast when his prodigal son returns. Not only that, but this same Father tells his obedient older son to *enjoy* his wealth. God loves to give, and He wants us to share in and participate in His generosity. Like a good Father, he has pointed out that He will reward the kind of behavior that is pleasing to Him.

Scripture is very clear that almsgiving in the spirit of charity is exceedingly good for us. My favorite passage on this comes from Tobit:

> Give alms from your possessions. Do not turn your face away from any of the poor, so that God's face will not be turned away from you. Give in proportion to what you own. If you have great wealth, give alms out of your abundance; if you have but little, do not be afraid to give alms even of that little. You will be storing up a goodly treasure for yourself against the day of adversity. For almsgiving delivers from death and keeps one from entering into Darkness. Almsgiving is a worthy offering in the sight of the Most High for all who practice it. (Tobit 4:7–11)

You don't have to fear accusations of preaching the Prosperity Gospel, selling indulgences, or trying to "buy your way into heaven." Preaching almsgiving follows directly on the way that Jesus preached the kingdom of God. You are standing on a firm foundation of Scripture and tradition. God wants us to practice generosity.

Blessings,
The Almoner

P.S. The true fruit of almsgiving can be seen in the spectacular beauty of St. Peter's Basilica where countless pilgrims have experienced an encounter with the Risen One and the Church that He founded. From one fundraiser to another, I thank Fr. Johann for his hard work and suffering.

7.

PLANNING WITH GOD IN MIND

Dear Fr. Zagloba,

THE THUNDERSTORM ON Sunday really shook the church. It reminded me that we need to talk about getting a new roof. We're not quite in the "putting out buckets" stage, but I don't think that's too far off.

Let's first admit that this is a problem you inherited. Your predecessor, Fr. Ryan, loved his parishioners, and his parishioners loved him. However, he did not keep up with the financial management side of things because that just wasn't his particular gift. That part of the plan was left out.

I'm not saying this as a mark against him. Look at the apostles. They started the diaconate so they could focus more on pastoring and less on administration. No one is good at everything.

Back to our situation. You now have the responsibility to raise the money to fix the roof and to take care of the multitude of other 'deferred maintenance' issues that are beginning to crop up. The finance council has started a list, and it is pretty long. Not to worry! God created everything out of nothing. Roofs and carpets are easy compared to that.

So where to start?

YES, FAITH AND PRUDENCE CAN WORK TOGETHER (WHEN YOU ARE PLANNING WITH GOD IN MIND)

Waiting to raise money for the roof until you need to put out buckets is kind of like waiting until the house is on fire to blow out the candles on your birthday cake. Small problems can become enormous disasters very quickly. That is why planning is so important.

Fr. Ryan used to say that we just had to have faith that God would provide the money when we needed it. I think he is correct in principle, but I disagree with his approach.

Faith and prudence can (and really should) work together. Faith says that God can provide. "My God will fully supply whatever you need, in accord with his glorious riches in Christ Jesus" (Philippians 4:19). Prudence says that planning and saving money to pay for repairs is an effective way to avoid a constant state of crisis. Jesus pointed out the need for prudent planning:

> Which of you wishing to construct a tower does not first sit down and calculate the cost to see if there is enough for its completion? Otherwise, after laying the foundation and finding himself unable to finish the work the onlookers should laugh at him and say, "This one began to build but did not have the resources to finish." (Luke 14:28–32)

The book of Proverbs puts a little sharper point on it. I love how blunt Proverbs can be sometimes:

> Go to the ant, O sluggard, study her ways and learn wisdom; For though she has no chief, no commander or ruler, she procures her food in the summer, stores up her provisions in the harvest. How long, O sluggard, will you lie there? When will you rise from your sleep? A little sleep, a little slumber, a little folding of the arms to rest—Then poverty will come upon you like a robber, and want like a brigand. (Proverbs 6:6–11)

These passages point out that the life of faith does not eliminate the need for prudent planning, diligence, and industry. In fact, they point out that God will allow us to suffer the consequences of our failure to plan. God wants us to be faithful AND prudent.

An example of this from my own life …

My wife and I drive old cars. I'm a food banker, not an investment banker. They're paid off, but they break down from time to time. As a precaution, I pull a small amount from every paycheck and set it aside for car repair.

A while ago, the radiator on my truck blew up, and it was going to cost $500 to fix it. I checked our 'car repair' account, and it had $510 saved up. No crisis. God provided $50 a month for ten months to give me the money that I needed to fix my truck at the exact moment that I needed it.

WE'RE NOT JUST REBUILDING BUILDINGS; WE'RE REBUILDING TRUST

Fixing a roof is not a capital campaign. A capital campaign is building something new that excites people. Roof repair is raising money to pay for deferred maintenance, so it requires a different approach.

It's kind of hard to get people excited about fixing the roof, especially since it has been an obvious need for such a long time.

Maybe when we're planning our next fundraiser, we should start with laying out a new vision for maintaining the parish. People loved Fr. Ryan, so they forgave the fact that the grounds weren't taken care of and that the buildings were starting to show their age.

But this is their church. If you ask people, they'll tell you that they got discouraged watching the church disintegrate. With this knowledge, you will want to be prudent and set up the right structures that guarantee the parish is well taken care of in the future.

Speaking of prudence, my wife is calling me to dinner. Listening to the call is prudent. If I have any more ideas about how we should approach the roof, I'll drop you another line.

Blessings,
The Almoner

8.

OPENING THE EYES OF THE BLIND

Dear Fr. Zagloba,

YOU'RE RIGHT, FATHER, rebuilding trust takes time. It won't happen overnight. However, the first thing to focus on is to help people see where we are going, together, as a parish.

VISION, VISION, VISION, VISION, VISION

The key to all of this is that people need to see where you are leading them. Think of how obvious God made it for the Israelites when He led them by a pillar of cloud in the daytime and a pillar of flame at night. They knew the drill. If the pillar moved, they moved. If it stopped, they stopped.

You don't have the benefit of a giant flaming pillar, so you're going to have to paint the picture yourself, in your homilies and announcements.

Think of these five steps as a road map that will lead to a revitalized parish.

STEP 1—START WITH THE "BIG VISION."

Our parish is our little corner of God's kingdom. It is a place of encounter between the King of Creation and a hungry world.

We need to focus on the divine mission of the Church: to baptize, to make disciples of the nations, and to instruct them in living as Jesus commanded.

By doing so, you can get everyone fired up about the supernatural incredibleness of the life of faith. You demonstrate to your parishioners their important roles of making that life of faith a reality, right here, right now, in our community.

The Church exists to evangelize and to bring new people into the family of God. If our parish begins to understand and live that out fully, it will really come alive.

STEP 2—GIVE PEOPLE A VISION THAT INCLUDES THEM

You need to help people see that the Church is not just something "out there" but a vital part of their life. You should shake them out of being complacent pew potatoes and stir them to action. The action can be internally focused or directed outwards.

Internally focused action would include clubs or committees that help with needs at the Church. For instance, we need a "Handyman Club" to track the repairs of the church and to solicit bids from professionals and craftsmen. A garden club could mow the grass, plant flowers, weed, and beautify the landscape.

Externally focused action means getting our people involved in the corporal and spiritual works of mercy out in the community. So, volunteer teams to help at the soup kitchen, people to visit shut-ins, evangelization teams, and service teams would fall into this part of the vision.

These are not just activities for the sake of activity. You need help administering to the needs of the parish. The office of the diaconate was created in the early Church to manage administrative tasks for the Apostles to enable the leaders of the Church to fulfill their roles as preachers, teachers, and intercessors.

Helping people to discover how to use their gifts for the good of the Church and the community will bring new life to the parish. People want to feel like they're involved in something bigger than themselves, something good. They will be happier using their gifts to build God's kingdom and make it beautiful.

And you should not be mowing the lawn when you could be weeding souls in the confessional. Let the garden club do what they do best, which is making the entrance way beautiful. While they do this, you can do what you do best: beautify the souls of our community.

STEP 3—LAY OUT THE VISION OF ALL THE SHORT-TERM WORK TO BE DONE

Let's start with the BIG 3 ISSUES and then move down the list. The roof is first, then the potholes in the parking lot, then renovating the bathrooms. We can discuss the order of these three priorities with the Pastoral Council along with other input they have.

Also, I recommend you select a few SMALL ISSUES like touching up the paint on the wall next to the confessional which can be quick wins. These are small, but quick wins can create momentum. They are small, visible projects that won't take a HUGE amount of money, but once completed will be a visible sign that something is actually getting done.

A big part of building trust is delivering on the promises you make.

STEP 4—PROVIDE A VISION OF LONG-TERM FINANCIAL HEALTH FOR THE PARISH

We don't have to do everything at once. Honestly, we can't. We don't have the resources.

By starting with the BIG 3 ISSUES, the top three capital projects, you can focus your attention on raising funds for these specific projects. Don't get sidetracked by distractions along the way. Unless something blows up or catches fire, these will be your fundraising priorities.

As part of a vision for long term stability, we could start to place some funds into savings in case of an emergency. You could even say this is a fourth capital project. The Church needs a reserve that can handle emergencies should they arise. We'll need to discuss what our target amount should be, and you may need to discuss it with the diocese. It's going to take more than the

$50 I put aside for my cars every month to build up an emergency fund, but we should set a savings goal and shoot for it.

In fundraising, being specific about what is required and why it is needed is important. If people know how much we aim to raise and see our continual commitment to reaching those goals, the campaign will build momentum and finish strongly.

STEP 5—GO BACK TO THE BIG VISION

How does this all tie in with the mission of the Church in the world and our lives?

People give to causes that inspire and excite them, and the job of saving souls is always more exciting than fixing roofs.

However, by fixing the roof we have a place where we may worship the God of all creation in a way that honors and glorifies Him.

We are also making the church more accommodating to welcome the new people that our evangelization teams bring in to visit the parish. Exciting times are ahead!

REMEMBER, YOU CAN'T BE A BLIND GUIDE

"Without a vision, the people perish" (Proverbs 29:18). If you give them a vision, the people will 'Parish.' Couldn't resist the pun. Seriously, though, it's so important that you help our parishioners see the bigger picture, even while including enough detail so they can understand their role.

You can find an excellent example of this kind of fundraising in the Old Testament. Who led the first recorded capital campaign? None other than Moses, nemesis of Pharaoh, author of the Pentateuch, leader of the Israelites, and friend of God.

Moses and his followers wandered through the desert, and God gave him a vision for the tent of the Holy Presence and the tabernacle. God did not generalize in His instructions. He gave them very exacting specifics:

> The LORD spoke to Moses: Speak to the Israelites: Let them receive contributions for me. From each you shall receive the contribution that their hearts prompt them to give me. These are the contributions you shall accept from them: gold, silver, and bronze; violet, purple, and scarlet yarn; fine linen and goat hair; rams' skins dyed red, and tahash skins; acacia wood; oil for the light; spices for the anointing oil and for the fragrant incense; onyx stones and other gems for mounting on the ephod and the breastpiece. They are to make a sanctuary for me, that I may dwell in their midst. According to all that I show you regarding the pattern of the tabernacle and the pattern of its furnishings, so you are to make it. (Exodus 25:1–9)

God's instructions continue for another six chapters.

When Moses explains the vision to the people, they give to him with such generosity that he is forced to tell them to stop giving. If only every capital campaign were so successful!

These chapters point to the primacy of prayer and give us an inspiring model for fundraising. It was not just Moses's vision that stirred everyone to give. God provided the vision. Infused with God's divine inspiration, Moses had the clarity to articulate the plan.

The more closely you align your vision to God's vision for St. Catherine's Parish, the more successful this entire process will be. And who knows, God might very well surprise you. He may have even bigger plans for the parish than we expect.

Spend some time praying about it. Ask the Lord to give you the vision that He wants you to share with his people. I look forward to hearing what the Lord has planned.

Blessings,
The Almoner

9.

KNOCK! KNOCK! WHO'S THERE? BEN HUR!

Dear Fr. Zagloba,

SORRY, WE MISSED YOU. We went to St. Jude's for Mass last weekend to hear my sister-in-law cantor. That church is the jewel of the city. Our boys just loved looking up at traditional stained-glass windows. The incense, the Gregorian Chant. It's quite heavenly. I think the beauty of the church helped them to focus.

So, it turned out that the focus of the sermon and the announcements was St. Jude's annual stewardship campaign. The Gospel reading was the parable of the unjust steward:

> Then he also said to his disciples, "A rich man had a steward who was reported to him for squandering his property. He summoned him and said, 'What is this I hear about you? Prepare a full account of your stewardship, because you can no longer be my steward.' The steward said to himself, 'What shall I do, now that my master is taking the position of steward away from me? I am not strong enough to dig and I am ashamed to beg. I know what I shall do so that, when I am removed from the stewardship, they may welcome me into their homes.' He called in his master's debtors one by one. To the first he said, 'How much do you owe my master?' He replied, 'One hundred measures of olive oil.' He said to him, 'Here is your promissory note. Sit down and quickly write one for fifty.' Then to another he said, 'And you, how much do you owe?' He replied, 'One hundred kors of wheat.' He said to him, 'Here is your promissory note; write one for eighty.' And the master commended that dishonest steward for acting prudently. For the children of this world are more prudent in dealing with their own generation than are the children of light. I tell you, make friends for yourselves with dishonest (unjust) wealth, so that when it fails, you will be welcomed into eternal dwellings." (Luke 16:1–9)

I was hopeful when I realized that this was the launching point for our stewardship homily. It seemed like a natural starting point for the campaign, but boy, was I wrong.

WHAT ARE YOU PUTTING IN THE MAILBOX?

Why does every stewardship homily talk about how much it costs to keep the church air-conditioned? I mean really. I know this is Georgia and that we should probably start a Saint's cause for whoever invented air conditioning, but is this the best topic to get people inspired to give?

NO! Air conditioning bills just aren't exciting. Do you get excited when you get the Georgia Power Bill? Mine is much smaller than the parish's, but even so, I don't race to the mail box every month filled with hope that maybe, just maybe, the power bill has arrived.

Think about the things that thrill you when you open your mailbox. Letters from a friend? Birthday cards? Something unexpected? Or maybe it's that book that you've been waiting for that has been on back order? When something that we've been waiting for shows up in the mailbox, we get a thrill because IT'S FINALLY HERE.

When you open your mailbox and see that it's full, you get a little excited, don't you? That excitement drains away like a bathtub when you realize that it's nothing but bills and ads. The same thing can happen when you start your stewardship campaign with a discussion of just how much it costs to keep the build in g air c on d *zzzz* ZZZZZ ZZZZZZ ZZZZZ ZZZZ. By the end of your first paragraph, people are dead in the pews.

AIM FOR SIZZLE, NOT FIZZLE!

Have you ever read the book, *Ben Hur?* Not the movies, although the one with Charlton Heston may be one of the best films ever made. The book captures something that just doesn't show up on the big screen. Longing. Deep and desperate hunger. For the Messiah. The whole book centers on this national desire for the arrival of the Messiah. Conversations about 'the Galilean' focus on this question—"Who is he ... ? Is he the one promised by the prophets?"

Every conversation in that book sizzled with anticipation. That's our aim. When you talk about stewardship, parish life, outreach ... it should be like throwing a handful of steak strips in a hot cast iron skillet. SIZZLE. The kingdom God is exciting!!! It is supernaturally exciting, and our Parish is on the front lines. The time of fulfillment is at hand. The kingdom of God is among us!

In a very tangible way, stewardship lets us participate in fulfilling the Our Father's 'on earth as it is in heaven.' Doesn't this get you excited? Think about how you felt when you first entered the seminary, ready to give up everything to serve God and build His Church. The sacrifices you made were real, and they were difficult, but God gave you the hunger to "Go therefore and make disciples of all nations ..." (Matthew 28:19). And you willingly left everything behind.

That hunger, the—"I'll leave everything to follow You, Jesus,"—that's the sizzle. If you're not feeling it at this moment, dive into prayer. Ask God to rekindle that fire in you. As St. Catherine of Siena, our church's patron, famously said, "Be who God created you to be, and you will set the world on fire!"

You are a priest of the Most High God! WOW! Through the sacraments, you bring people into real, physical, spiritual contact with the Creator of all things. Focus fully on this reality, pushing every urgent but fruitless distraction to the side, and there's no telling what will happen. In a year, we could be planning a capital campaign to accommodate all our new parishioners.

GOD'S WAYS ARE NOT THE WORLD'S WAYS

The parable of the unjust steward can be the perfect introduction to a stewardship campaign. Ultimately, the parable is about mortality and eternity. Our time on this Earth will come to an end, and we need to have an eternal perspective on our material possessions. Everything we own comes from the Lord, and when we go to meet our Maker, they all go to someone else. As Job famously says, "The Lord gave and the Lord has taken away" (Job 1:21).

I've often wondered about why the master praised his steward for what seemed to me like stealing from him. Then it hit me. "Forgive us our debts as we forgive our debtors." The dishonest steward was being unjust, in the sense that he was forgiving the debts justly accrued by his master's debtors. His master was not praising him for dishonesty, but for his generosity. He was being merciful to the debtors, in the hopes that he would receive mercy when he got ousted from his position.

Good stewardship is precisely defined as the prudent use of money and material goods. The problem we face in the Church is that the Jesus has a very different idea of what prudent management looks like than the world does. The world says, "Loan and get your principle back with interest." Jesus says "lend expecting nothing back" (Luke 6:35). Prudent stewardship in the kingdom of God doesn't cling to wealth and possessions the way the world does. It teaches us to always keep our mind on our eternal destiny.

The final verses of the Gospel reading can open our eyes to understand the way that God wants us to view wealth and material possessions:

> The person who is trustworthy in very small matters is also trustworthy in great ones; and the person who is dishonest in very small matters is also dishonest in great ones. If, therefore, you are not trustworthy with dishonest wealth, who will trust you with true wealth? If you are not trustworthy with what belongs to another, who will give you what is yours? No servant can serve two masters. He will either hate one and love the other, or, be devoted to one and despise the other. You cannot serve God and mammon. (Luke 16:10–13)

Jesus wants to entrust to us true wealth, eternal treasure in the kingdom of God, but first He uses small matters to form our hearts. The way that we treat money and material possessions have a profound impact on our ability to serve God. Jesus wants our hearts detached from the unjust wealth of this world so that we can seek true wealth, which only comes from being a servant of the God. This kind of wealth never perishes, can never be stolen, and will last for eternity.

A SURPRISE INHERITANCE, NOT UTILITY BILLS OR TAX NOTICES

When you talk about stewardship, you don't want to focus on the boring but necessary details of what it costs to keep the parish running. You don't want to leave the parishioners the idea that their gifts are mandatory or without merit. Instead, you're inviting them to claim their inheritance as children of God. Our stewardship campaign should be one of the most exciting parts of our parish life because it means helping them to be faithful in small things so God can entrust them with big things. You are calling them to serve the Lord with every part of their lives, and the rewards are eternal! Exciting stuff!

Blessings,
The Almoner

P.S. Would you like to come over to dinner Wednesday night? Mary is making something that is tasteless and bland. We will be bored senseless.

P.P.S. See how that doesn't work? Let's try it again. Want to join us for dinner Wednesday night? Mary is making pot roast with all the fixin's, and I think I can convince her to whip up a homemade chocolate cheesecake with raspberry sauce. If you're up for it, afterwards we can go out back, and I'll teach you how to throw knives.

10.

MAJOR GIFTS FOR BEGINNERS—PART ONE

Dear Fr. Zagloba,

THAT'S TERRIBLE NEWS!

I thought the technician told you we could get another two years out of that furnace. I'm sorry, Father. You don't need this right after Christmas.

I agree with you that we shouldn't empty out our "rainy day fund," at least not yet. I think maybe God is giving you an opportunity to "put out into the deep." Maybe we can try some major gift fundraising.

WHAT IS MAJOR GIFT FUNDRAISING?

Major gifts fundraising starts with the idea that it takes less effort to ask for $10,000 once than it does to ask for $5 two thousand times. To succeed, you just need to ask the right people, at the right time, in the right way.

You don't have to have full-time fundraising staff to succeed at major gifts, although you'll find that this is where most top-level fundraising organizations focus the bulk of their energy and resources. I'm going to lead you through a beginner's approach to major gifts that will be manageable with the time, energy, and urgency that you face in the current situation.

START WITH THE RIGHT PEOPLE

Major gift requests can give even the most hardened fundraiser a case of the cold sweats, but I don't think this will be all that bad.

Fixing the furnace will cost $43,000. I just got a grant for exactly that amount, so I know that this is doable.

A few major gifts should be enough to take care of this whole problem. We just need to be asking people who can give sizeable donations.

STEP 1—GETTING ORGANIZED

The first step is to ask Carmen to pull a report of the top 30 donors from the past year. It may sound counter-intuitive, but study after study shows that your biggest gifts will come from your biggest givers. Why? Because they already support the Church at an elevated level, and they will respond warmly to a personal request for a big gift.

Even if they have to say no, they'll feel honored that you thought that they would be able to make a larger contribution. These parishioners also are likely not to give you the cold shoulder or interrogate you.

STEP 2—BOOK APPOINTMENTS

The next step is to take your list and make 30 phone calls. I recommend you do this yourself. You may have to call multiple times because you should not leave voice mails asking for donations. Asking is always best done in person.

When you call, just say, "Hello, this is Fr. Zagloba from St. Catherine's. First off, I want to thank you for being such a huge supporter of the church. I'm calling to see if you can help me. I have an unexpected problem to start the year: the furnace has gone up in smoke. I'd appreciate if I could speak to you in person. When on [pick a day or two as options] would you be able to have a cup of coffee [or tea or lunch] with me?"

If you do have to leave a voice message, only say, "Hello, this is Fr. Zagloba from St. Catherine's. When you have a moment, please give me a call at [phone number]. Thank you, and may God bless you."

Aim to make 30 appointments to meet with each parishioner individually. Give yourself at least 45 minutes to one hour to meet with them. Yes, raising this kind of money requires a significant time commitment. By investing the time to meet and speak with them individually, you are giving your parishioners the kind of attention that a big gift deserves. You will get more gifts by asking in person, and you will also be building relationships with some of the most dedicated members of the parish.

STEP 3—THE TOUGH PART

When you have a parishioner (either alone or with their spouse), I recommend you take the time to reconnect with them. Take this excellent opportunity to learn how they are doing. After a hot cup of coffee, explain to them that the furnace has gone up in smoke, literally and that it will cost $43,000 to replace it. Ask them to prayerfully consider if they can make a gift of $1,000—$5,000 to contribute to making the replacement possible.

I suggest using open questions, such as, "Would you be willing to consider making a gift in the $1–5,000 range?" Open questions offer parishioners the opportunity to share more openly their thoughts. Closed questions, such as "Will you" or "Can you," don't offer parishioners the time or space to think because you are immediately moving them to a yes/no decision.

Repeat this process 30 times. Chances are some people will say no. Other people will say yes. Yes, it's always possible that one or two will say, "How dare you to ask me?" The first group won't hurt you, the second will bless you, and the third will give you an opportunity to thank them and praise them for their current generosity profusely.

STEP 4—COMPELLING STORIES WORK

Father Zagloba, this will work better than you expect. Will it raise all $43,000? More than likely, although even if you fall short of the goal, it will take a huge bite out of the total bill and preserve most of the rainy-day fund.

And yes, I think we have a good reason not to take the easy route and just drain the bank account. An engaging story, a compelling need, this is the fundraiser's "silver bullet." It often makes the impossible a reality.

I have an Uncle from Canada who travels with his family doing praise and worship concerts. They go all over the place in their RV, sometimes going to two or three different cities in a week. They badly needed to replace their dilapidated transportation. But try as they might, they couldn't raise nearly enough money to get a new one.

Then one day the wheels fell off. Literally. They were traveling on the west coast of Canada, 3,000 miles from home, and the rear axle broke off. They were stranded, and the RV wasn't worth repairing. They got on email and social media and showed photos of the broken axle. They explained the need and the fact that they were stranded. Without the money to fix the RV, they could not go home.

And by gum, it worked. Within a week and a half, my uncle and his family were back on the road in a brand-new RV paid for in cash. We're talking more than $100,000.

GOD IS IN CHARGE!

Father, you just need to tell your story. For the big gifts we need, you should do it face to face with individuals. You'll tell the story from the pulpit for sure, but you simply can't beat one-on-one, eye-to-eye contact when you're asking for a big gift.

What a story! A whiff of smoke leads you into the basement. You practically choke when you get down there, the smoke is so thick. You see the fire in the furnace wiring, and put it out with the new fire extinguisher that you installed a few weeks ago as part of your new program of taking care of deferred maintenance issue. You were in the right place, at the right time. Thanks be to God.

Thanks to God's providence and some quick thinking, we do not have to build a new church, or even worse, bury our priest.

What's $43,000 compared to that? Nothing. Thank You, Jesus!

Blessings,
The Almoner

11.

MAJOR GIFTS FOR BEGINNERS—PART TWO

Dear Fr. Zagloba,

THAT'S AWESOME! Don't worry, we set the bar high, and this is a great result. Five one-on-one meetings in your first week? Six more scheduled for next week? Two gift commitments already? Fantastic. That's $6,000 you didn't have a week ago.

Only $37,000 more to go.

So, here's what you might want to do now. The heat is on (figuratively) because the heat is off (in actuality). We do need a new furnace immediately. You should continue the major gift requests in the coming weeks, as hard as it is, but now you have new arrows in your quiver.

IT'S TIME FOR 'FOLLOW THE LEADER.'

This Sunday is the first that everyone in the parish will hear about (and experience) the death of the furnace. Even though it is consuming all your attention right now, most of the parish has no idea. I think that you can use the two gifts that you have already secured to help raise most, if not all the rest, of the money relatively quickly.

At the end of Mass, you can tell the story about how, by God's providence, you were able to prevent the furnace from burning down the church with its dying breath. Then tell the parishioners about how two donors have already stepped up and committed to funding $6,000 of the $43,000 that it will cost to replace it. Be grateful for their generosity and thank them. (You don't have to mention their names, but I'll get into more detail about this further in the letter.)

Then ask your parishioners to consider donating to help replace the furnace. The gift commitments that you have already gotten should be one of the focal points of your announcement. "Why?" you ask? Because people always follow the leader.

GREAT(ER) EXPECTATIONS

When you tell us that you are raising money to buy a new furnace, people will initially think, "Well, how much cash do I have in my wallet?" That is great, don't get me wrong. But two-hundred $20 gifts only bring in another $4,000. It simply isn't going to be enough. It's less than the two donations that you have so far.

When you tell people that two of their fellow parishioners have already given $6,000, it will completely recalibrate their 'give-o-meter.' Even if they can't make a $1,000+ gift, you're setting much higher expectations and opening their eyes to the idea of making a big donation. They might give $100-$500 instead of $20.

One word of caution. In a big public setting like the Mass announcements, the donors should be anonymous. Remember, Jesus warned us:

> But take care not to perform righteous deeds in order that people may see them; otherwise, you will have no recompense from your heavenly Father. When you give alms, do not blow a trumpet before you, as the hypocrites do in the synagogues and in the streets to win the praise of others. Amen, I say to you, they have received their reward. But when you give alms, do not let your left hand know what your right is doing, so that your almsgiving may be secret. And your Father who sees in secret will repay you. (Matthew 6:1–4)

What Jesus says here is important. One of the topics that I've been harping on is the spiritual benefit that comes as the result of giving to the Church and to the poor. If we encourage our donors to "blow their own trumpets," we're leading them astray and stealing any spiritual benefit that they might have received. If you refer to the gifts without naming the donor, you're encouraging additional big gifts without doing any damage to the original donor's spiritual life.

SEND FORTH YOUR DISCIPLES

Your two major donors might be able to serve in another way by helping you with your face-to-face asks. There's an old fundraising proverb, "Donors give to givers." It makes sense if you think about it. If I'm asking you to give to a cause, and I can tell you that I've already made a significant gift to that cause, my request will be more credible. You are more likely to give when someone you know has given.

The scenario works especially well with larger gifts. If I've given $100, and I ask you to give $5,000, some part of you will think, "Who does this bozo think he is?" If, however, I gave $10,000, and I ask you to give $5,000, you might think, "Wow, he's generous. I want to be like him."

Asking someone face-to-face is different from getting up and announcing their gift. They aren't getting the big public glory that Jesus warns us to avoid. Instead, they will be privately asking people that they know to join them in making a substantial gift. Your donor can be discreet by referring to their gift as a "leadership gift" rather than giving a specific amount. If asked what qualifies as a leadership gift, they can say gifts $3,000 or above. (For future reference, the leadership gift range can change depending on how much money you're trying to raise.)

If the donors are agreeable, we'll ask them to come up with a list of five people in the parish whom they know are able to make a gift of $2–5,000. We'll coach them in doing the same kind of phone call, meeting set-up, and in-person ask that you've been doing. They know this fundraising approach works, because they've just given in response to your efforts.

If they're willing to do it, I think they'll succeed. Let me know what they say, and I'll get on the phone with them to coach them through the process.

Blessings,
The Almoner

P.S. By the way, a 40% success rate on asking for major gifts your first week is pretty much walking on water. You should be very encouraged. We'll have the heat back on in no time.

12.

MAJOR GIFTS FOR BEGINNERS—THE GRAND FINALE!

Dear Fr. Zagloba,

FANTASTIC NEWS! Who knew that you would be able to raise $29,000 in such a brief time? Having the right story and the right approach makes all the difference, doesn't it? I've been at the parish for nearly a decade, and we have never had a fundraising drive like this. Stop and think about the size of the bake sale needed to raise $29,000.

Inconceivable! It would be physically impossible for our parish to bake 58,000 brownies in two weeks. We don't have enough ovens! But you and one volunteer made it happen … just by asking! Hallelujah!

Sure, I don't see any problem with pulling the trigger on replacing the furnace right away with what we've already collected and closing any gap with the emergency reserve. I do think that if you do two more weeks of lunch meetings for major gifts and mention how close we are to the goal at the next several Masses, you'll raise the rest without any problems. You have momentum on your side.

PEOPLE JUMP ON MOVING TRAINS

You have blown everyone's expectations out of the water. If you had asked them a month ago if it were possible to raise $43,000, the parishioners probably would have laughed you out of the parish. Respectfully, of course, because they love you. But they would have thought you were crazy.

Now the game has changed. I expect several more sizable donations to come by Sunday, and you'll be able to tell everyone that you broke the $30,000 mark in under three weeks. This momentum will get even more people excited and encourage them to give more gifts, particularly at the lower levels. They will want to be a part of making this exciting moment happen.

People like to be a part of something successful. Even parishioners who are typically reluctant to get involved. When they see that the train is moving, they want to jump on and be a part of it. Who wants to miss out on doing that big event where everybody was involved? Nobody.

GET READY TO CELEBRATE

It could be a watershed moment for the parish. Let's find a clear spot on the schedule, and maybe next week you can announce that we are having a potluck or picnic to celebrate. We should organize an event that will thank the whole parish for responding to this fundraising drive, especially everyone who may have just given the biggest gifts EVER to the Church. The celebration doesn't have to be fancy, just soon.

Why? One thing that jumps out to donors is showing the right amount of attention to say, "thank you." Here's a straightforward way you can do this. Ask Mr. Jenson if the Knights of Columbus will sponsor coffee and donuts after the 10 AM Mass in two weeks for a "Thank You" celebration. You can have the parish pay for it and ask the Knights to the legwork. They made several of the biggest gifts, so they should be happy to help. We have got to celebrate. You should make a big deal about this.

This major 'crisis' might just become a turning point for this parish. You are changing the way the parishioners think about St. Catherine's. The difference between being the kind of parish that raises $400 from a bake sale and the one that can raise $40,000 in less than a month is incredible.

The way they perceive themselves, you, this Church, the mission of the Church, can be transformed by this event. Rather than everyone thinking we're just a "sleepy little Catholic Church on the buckle of the Bible Belt," we can think of ourselves as "that resourceful little Catholic Church that just did something BIG."

"ALL THINGS WORK TOGETHER FOR GOOD FOR THOSE WHO LOVE GOD AND ARE CALLED ACCORDING TO HIS PURPOSES."
(ROMANS 8:28)

And here's the big lesson. God is in charge. Fundraising might have been one of your least favorite things that you've had to do as a priest. I understand. Major gifts fundraising is hard for professionals. But God gave you an opportunity to step out of your comfort zone, and you did it. Even more, it paid off. I think it's just great.

The next step after the "thank you" donuts is to figure out what to do with this new momentum. Let's pray about it and see where the Lord leads us.

Blessings,
The Almoner

P.S. I know it's cheesy, but the old classic 'Fundraising thermometer' might work to help take this over the top. It's a good visual for people who haven't yet given to see how their gift can make a difference. Since we're already 3/4 of the way to the top, I think it will be an encouragement to receive those last few gifts.

Plus, use blue ink. We are raising money for a furnace, and it will point out the fact that it's COLD in there. Write the headline, "Turn on the Heat!" above the thermometer. It's just too perfect.

13.

THE RICH MAN AND LAZARUS—
A PARADIGM FOR FUNDRAISING

Dear Fr. Zagloba,

I'LL LET MARY KNOW that you loved the cheesecake. We wanted to do something special to celebrate the new furnace. Praise the Lord that the heat's back on.

I have been thinking about a comment you made on your way out. You're right. The parable of the rich man and Lazarus is a doozy. In our money obsessed culture, it's like a landmine. People, preachers especially, twist and contort themselves to avoid stepping on it. They're terrified that it will blow up in their faces. They think people simply won't listen to a message that contradicts the American doctrine that more cars, more houses, and more money mean more happiness. But we can't ignore what Jesus said. So how do we understand it? How should we let it inform our fundraising?

SEE PEOPLE WITH NEW EYES

After you left, Mary and I discussed the parable further ... which character in the story is the most wretched, the most in need of God's mercy? Think about it. Lazarus suffers terribly for what feels like a long time but then goes on to eternal consolation. He only experiences a "momentary and light affliction when compared with the weight of eternal glory" (2 Corinthians 4:17).

Now, look at the rich man. He has everything that he desires in this life but pays the penalty of eternal suffering for neglecting Lazarus. In the balance of eternity, his misery far outweighs Lazarus's. Jesus specifically points this out when He says, "Woe to you who are rich now, for you have received your consolation" (Luke 6:24). Jesus said this for a reason, and I think fundraisers need to consider it very carefully.

FUNDRAISING FOR THE KINGDOM IS ALL ABOUT MERCY

When you're moving on to your next big fundraising project (fixing the Church roof), God's mercy is probably not at the top of your mind. Unless you are asking God, in His mercy, to deliver you from fundraising. But you need to recognize that fundraising is a ministry to the rich (and the middle class) in the same way that a soup kitchen is a ministry to the poor. It meets them in their need for God's mercy.

"Blessed are the merciful, for they shall receive mercy" (Matthew 5:7). You know that the word alms comes from the Greek word for mercy. By inviting your "rich man" to be a donor, you are encouraging him to be merciful. His generous response opens the door for him to receive God's mercy. He may or may not know that he is needs God's mercy, but the parable points out how enormous that need may be.

Remember the parable. Abraham tells the rich man that Lazarus would have been satisfied with the scraps from his table. A few boxes of leftovers would have made the difference between eternal beatitude and unquenchable fire. By encouraging mercy in the rich, you may very well be saving them from perdition.

Modern fundraising techniques can be very useful in this process. Packaging your capital project with nice materials and clear budgets helps people to decide to do good. You're asking them to do something that has a direct, and potentially eternal, spiritual benefit. Almsgiving is life-giving … medicine for the soul.

CHEESECAKE, NOT BRUSSEL SPROUTS

The way we approach our potential donors is still very important. If Mary had made the cheesecake with brussels sprouts, it might have been healthier, but you wouldn't have eaten a second piece. Or a last sliver. Or taken some home.

Remember in the parable how the rich man begged Abraham to send someone to his brothers to warn them of the suffering that awaits them. You get to be that messenger, but not by preaching gloom and doom and the danger of falling into hell. Jesus said that approach wouldn't work even if someone rose from the dead. In other words, the brussels sprouts won't sell the cheesecake.

You need to focus on the "cheesecake" approach to almsgiving. Help the members of our parish to see themselves as generous stewards of God's many gifts. Show them that it's exciting to build God's kingdom. Enable them to experience the fun of serving the community. Their gift can make a huge difference in people's lives.

The cheesecake will bring them back again and again. Give the medicine of almsgiving a chance to change their lives. Every gift that they give to the Church and the poor is *a practical act of conversion.* And not because you have frightened them to death of the punishments of hell, but because you have shared with them the delights of heaven. Empower them to be cheerful givers. Fundraising at its best is teaching others the joy of giving.

This parable provides the key ingredient of the cheesecake because it can transform the way you look at fundraising. It helps you to recognize that our biggest priority is not reaching a monetary goal but filling the kingdom of heaven with as many people as we can convince to come with us. Do we love the poor because they're poor? Or because they're people? Do we love the rich because they're rich? Or because they're people? Poor and rich alike, all fall short of the glory of God and need more of God's mercy.

DON'T FALL INTO THE SOCIAL JUSTICE TRAP

One final thought on this parable. Understood wrongly, it can lead us into the social justice trap that says that the primary role of the Church is to alleviate physical poverty. I can say this because I've been raising money to feed the hungry for the last seven years. Serving the poor will always be a high priority, and well it should be because Jesus points out the penalty for neglect. But it is not the highest priority.

Love of God is a higher-order commandment than the love of neighbor. Remember Mary anointed Jesus' feet before the Crucifixion using her costly alabaster jar of perfumed ointment. Jesus approved of this act of worship and specifically pointed out that it was better than selling the ointment to serve the poor. The worship of God is the highest use of any material good. Also, the greatest poverty, the most terrible wretchedness that exists in this life, or the next for that matter, is separation from God. Evangelism is a ministry to the poor in spirit. Building a vibrant, active, and evangelistic parish life is the only way to minister to those who know the spiritual poverty of not having faith, hope, and love.

Social justice is good, but without Divine Justice, it's just Marxism. Any altruistic heathen can provide bread to the hungry. Only a priest of Jesus Christ can bring them the Bread of Life. The Church is supernatural, and we have supernatural delights that won't fit into the materialist's narrow and corrupted understanding. Eucharistic adoration, beautiful liturgy, evangelism, faith formation … these feed the hunger of the part of each person that is eternal and most dearly needs God's mercy.

The power of this parable lies in the way it teaches us to look at each person, rich or poor: with an eternal perspective. Everyone needs the mercy and the hope that only the Church in all its fullness can provide. God has prepared a banquet for all men to feast for all eternity. You get to deliver the invitations.

Blessings,
The Almoner

P.S. We both know several very wealthy, very generous people. They prove the point I'm trying to make. Their immense joy in giving is the fruit of the love of God that they express through their generosity.

14.

TIME, TALENT, AND THE FISH WITH A GOLDEN TOOTH

Dear Fr. Zagloba,

I JUST FINISHED A BOOK that you might like. It could be a good read for the Pastoral Council. We could discuss it in depth together. It is called *Grateful and Giving* by Deacon Don McArdle. He founded a company called Catholic Stewardship Consultants that specifically focuses on training parishes how to do "stewardship." He starts with the story of the person who seems to have started the whole "Time, Talent, and Treasure" ball rolling.

If you're like me, you've never heard of Msgr. Thomas McGread. He served in the Diocese of Wichita, Kansas. Early in his priesthood, he searched for a theological foundation for the financial aspects of running his parish. In the early days of his priesthood, the priests typically asked their people to "give until it hurts." Msgr. McGread didn't like it and thought that there must be a better way. He stumbled on a book written about tithing, and this helped him see that the best reason to give to the Church is as a response to God's loving generosity to us.

I don't know if he's the one who coined the phrase, "Time, Talent, and Treasure," but he used it to knock the ball out of the park. He didn't focus on the offertory. He didn't want people to give money to the Church and sit like blobs in the pews for an hour on Sunday. He wanted them to invest their lives in the parish. To get involved. To BE disciples. And to steward their time, talent, and treasure so that God gets His fair share FIRST.

It worked like gangbusters. It worked so well, in fact, that it transformed the whole diocese. It later served as the inspiration for the United States Conference of Catholic Bishop's letter, "Stewardship: A Disciple's Response."

GOOD DISCIPLES ARE GOOD STEWARDS

Msgr. McGread rightly focused on forming his parishioners into Catholic disciples and got them excited about participating in the mission of the Church. He used the call for "time, talent, and treasure" to get people involved in doing big things for Jesus. Or small things, for that matter, as long as it was SOMETHING. As people got more involved, they also began to preach tithing of income—giving of your "first fruits" to God and the Church. A remarkable thing happened … people listened and started getting involved and giving more.

At a certain point, his Bishop took notice and decided that the whole Diocese of Wichita was going to do stewardship the McGread way. On the last report, the Diocese is flourishing. They are opening instead of closing parochial schools, and all of them are free to students. "Stewardship" foots the bill for everyone who wants to attend. They have a tremendous number of vocations to the priesthood, as well as a significant number of ministries to the poor that are run by parishioners who volunteer.

To help take this vision and make it a reality at an individual church, Msgr. McGread used a very well developed and traditional fundraising process, the annual campaign, and gave it a supernatural focus.

CONTINUOUS RENEWAL

Msgr. McGread developed what the book calls the stewardship renewal campaign, which is what Deacon McArdle and his company help to set up in parishes new to the process. A campaign includes several different elements:

1. Regular preaching and teaching from the pulpit about what it means to be a disciple and how to live a stewardship lifestyle. Everything starts with calling people to live the Gospel more fully.

2. A monthly newsletter focused on stewardship that includes personal testimonies from people whose lives have been transformed by the stewardship way of life and practical ways to get involved.

3. An annual "ministry fair" where people can get acquainted with the different ministries offered at the parish.

4. A survey of parishioners to find out what needs exist that aren't currently being met by the parish.

5. A "stewardship committee" that helps the pastor to plan and execute the annual "Stewardship renewal campaign."

6. Annual retreats for church ministry leaders focusing on the spirituality of discipleship and stewardship.

7. Two testimony Sundays from active "steward" members of the parish, followed by Annual "Commitment Sunday." Everyone is asked to prayerfully commit to giving their time, talent, and treasure for the following year. Parishioners write down their commitment on pledge cards, which are collected by the stewardship committee. The leaders of the various ministries use the responses to get people involved. The office records financial pledges for follow-up.

Now, this isn't the only way to run an annual campaign, but it is both comprehensive and effective. We can think about which parts we want to use and how to add them to what we're doing.

THE PASTOR CALLS

Fr. Zagloba, you have a very special role to play in all of this. Remember when Jesus said, "My sheep listen to my voice: I know them, and they follow me" (John 10:27). As the pastor of this little sheepfold, you are His voice—Alter Christi. When you call to the sheep, they will listen and follow you, because you don't speak for yourself, but in Christ's Name.

Here is a critical point though—if you don't call them, they won't follow. If you don't invite your parishioners into a life of discipleship, who will? You have both the responsibility and the authority as their pastor. You are irreplaceable because you are standing in place of Christ as shepherd of the little flock at St. Catherine's.

Your mission is daunting, but also extremely exciting. It means that you are supernaturally empowered to call the members of our parish into a life of discipleship. What Jesus said contains a promise … when you call in His name, His sheep WILL follow you. A tremendous responsibility, but Pope Benedict XVI said, "We were not created for an easy life, but for great things, for goodness" (Pope Benedict XVI, 2005). The call to be a pastor is a call to something great—to lead your flock so that you fill the Church with new Saints. Powerful. St. John Vianney, pray for us.

THE FISH WITH THE GOLDEN TOOTH

I think Msgr. McGread and Deacon McArdle struck gold. Their approach to fundraising is to keep the "main thing" the "main thing." What do I mean by that?

One of my favorite incidents in the Gospel, just for its sheer supernatural weirdness, is when Jesus tells St. Peter to go fishing to get the money that he needs to pay the temple tax. St. Peter obeys and, behold, the fish that he catches has a gold coin stuck in its mouth that is sufficient to pay the tax (Matthew 17:24–27).

Now, if we take this to mean that we just need to go to the lake to find the funds we need for the new roof, I think we're headed in the wrong direction. When we look at this story, we need to understand the spiritual sense of the passage. Jesus called St. Peter to be a fisher of men. If he focused on being a "fisherman," an evangelist, then the resources that he needed would be in the mouth of the "fish" that he brought into the kingdom.

This passage is about keeping the main thing the main thing. The main thing for the parish is not to raise enough money to keep the lights on and put on a new roof. The main thing for our parish is to be a house of worship and prayer and to form our parishioners into missionary disciples and provide them with the spiritual nourishment that they need to live the Gospel fully. If St. Catherine's focuses on being what God intends, and doing what God commands, He will meet all our financial needs. That's what it means to catch a fish with a golden tooth.

Most importantly, St. Peter was focused on "fishing," not raising money. We can't just talk about stewardship as a way to increase our offertory. We must DO discipleship and stewardship, period. And trust that God will put the right fish on the line at the right time.

Blessings,
The Almoner

15.

NO BAKE FUNDRAISING

Dear Mrs. Sanderson,

I GOT SO EXCITED when Fr. Zagloba told me that you would like to start a food pantry here in the Parish. What a wonderful idea! You know as well as I do how many people in our neighborhood are struggling to make ends meet. I'm more than happy to help you get this ministry off the ground.

By the way, I want to apologize for the comment that I made during my first Pastoral Council Meeting about how it would take selling 185,000 brownies to pay for a new roof. Please forgive me if I offended you. I should have shared my concerns with you in private, but it's kind of a hot button topic for me.

LET'S START WITH A BUDGET

Fr. Zagloba told me that he fully supports the idea of a food pantry, but that the parish budget can't cover any additional cost. He will commit to finding an appropriate space in one of the parish buildings and to giving you time to do a second collection after Mass.

We need a source for the food you'll be giving out. I'll put you in touch with the person at the Food Bank who brings on new food pantries. She's a gem. You will just love her. The Food Bank will enable you distribute much more food with the money we will raise than if we tried to buy it retail.

Since you'll be rounding up volunteers to do all the work, food will be the major cost for the ministry. You can come up with a ballpark budget by plugging numbers into this equation:

(the number of families you want to serve each time you're open) X (the number of times you'll be open per month) X (the amount of food you want to provide each family) X (Estimated cost per pound of food) = (Monthly food budget for the pantry)

If you think you want to serve 40 families twice a month, providing 45 lbs. of food (roughly what a family of 4 eats in 3 days), at the cost of $1 per pound of food, you'll need about $3,600 per month. The big reason to use the Food Bank is that the average cost of food is much lower, between $0.15 and $0.25 per pound, which brings the cost to $540-$900 per month. These are manageable numbers for fundraising.

A BETTER WAY THAN BROWNIES

I'm going to suggest a fundraising technique called "Ministry Support Fundraising." Missionaries who are going into the field for an extended period often use this style of fundraising. They do not come back into town frequently, so they need people to commit to being long-term supporters.

With Fr. Zagloba's permission, we could start a club in the Parish called "The Pantry Partners." You become a Pantry Partner in one of two ways, by volunteering your time or by becoming a monthly donor to the Food Pantry. As we prepare to start the pantry, we'll ask people in the Parish to become Pantry Partners until we have monthly commitments to cover our target budget.

Once we have the details nailed down—where we will locate the food pantry, the budget, a partnership with the Food Bank—we'll do our "partner drive." One weekend, you'll get up after all the Masses and tell the story of the new food pantry, explain how much it is going to cost every month, and tell people how to become a "Pantry Partner." You'll focus on the fact that it is a long-term commitment, and how we're called by the Gospel to serve the hungry.

A sample script might be something like this:

Hello, everyone, I'm Norma Sanderson, and I've been a parishioner at St. Catherine's for 45 years. Thanks to Fr. Zagloba's encouragement and support,

I'm now leading the charge to start a food pantry to serve the hungry in our area. The food pantry will be open twice a month to start, and we'll need financial and volunteer support. We're starting the "Pantry Partners" club for people who commit to serve or donate every month. We hope to feed 80 families a month once we get started, and thanks to our local food bank, we'll be able to do that for around $1,000 per month. Please see me after Mass if you're interested, or call me. You can find my phone number in the bulletin.

ASK FOR WHAT YOU NEED

The ministry support approach will work better than you expect, especially if we commit to prayer before hand. God wants us to serve the poor, and so He will certainly move people to give according to their ability.

Jesus said, "Ask, and you shall receive." You plan on doing a noble thing. People will respond. Not everybody, but everybody you need to get this mission up and off the ground. After your first announcement, we can decide if we need to try another approach.

Blessings,
The Almoner

16.

DONATIONS, AND EYEBALLS, ONLINE

Dear Fr. Zagloba,

OVER THE WEEKEND, I thought about new ways that we can promote giving at the parish. Something jumped out at me like, "Duh, of course." Online giving. I looked at the website for the parish, which is terrible by the way, but I think you know that. I realized that the parish doesn't have any way to take online gifts. More importantly, there's no way for people to sign up for monthly recurring gifts from their credit card or checking account. Now, this may not seem like a huge deal, but we are missing a major opportunity.

MEET YOUR DONORS WHERE YOU FIND THEM!

I did a little bit of research, and it turns out that encouraging online giving can increase the monthly offertory by anywhere from 10–30%. Why is that? The research pointed out that the people who are giving want to give. But they forget. Or they go to another church for a wedding. Or they go out on vacation, especially during the summer. As a result, they typically only give on 40–45 out of 52 Sundays a year.

Online giving changes that. Donors can decide once, and their good intentions will be automatically carried out for the rest of the year. People do the same thing with the utility bills. I think the only checks that I write any more are my rent check and my weekly offering. Every Sunday it's always a bit dicey. I scramble to find my checkbook and write a check while trying to locate four clean shoes and put them on two toddlers. If we can get it set up, I'll be one of the first to enroll.

IF YOU BUILD IT, THEY WON'T COME

Also, it's not enough to just add online giving functionality to the website. Our website doesn't get much in the way of traffic. When was the last time you visited it? I think Carmen may be the only person who uses it regularly, and that's because she's responsible for updating it. We need a plan to promote the online giving through the website that is low impact and repeats itself over and over.

I suggest a few easy elements that can run on autopilot once we put them in place:

1. We can put a button with a link to the donation page on our website. Something eye-catching like one that says, "Tithe Today."

2. Then we'll add a blurb to the bulletin that has that same "Tithe Today" button and a brief explanation of the fact that we can now accept donations online.

3. At least for a couple of months, you need to mention the availability of online giving during the announcements after Mass. Not an ask, mind you, simply the statement, "You can now make your monthly tithe payment through recurring online donations."

4. And finally, I think you should add an "online giving" column to the weekly offertory report in the bulletin. Nothing motivates people to give like seeing other people giving.

WHAT'S IN THE BASKET?

I know that there will be some people who will say, "But I'll feel bad if I don't put something in the basket during the offertory." That's ok. You can reassure them that we will continue to pass the collection basket and they are more than welcome to give that way. We're simply providing people who are not particularly attached to the basket a convenient way to give.

Or you could suggest doing what my wife and I are doing. I bring $1 bills to give to each of my sons to teach them the importance of giving to the church, but my main gift would be drafted automatically every month. The convenience is priceless. Ultimately, I will end up giving substantially MORE every year than I used to give. I just finished doing my taxes, and when I looked at my gift receipt from St. Catherine's, I realized that I will give at least 10% more when I can donate through a monthly recurring gift.

With your permission, I'd be happy to start working with Carmen on getting this up and running.

Blessings,
The Almoner

P.S. Letting people know that the church can accept online gifts does not get you off the hook for preaching on the importance of tithing. They mutually support each other, but they are two distinct and important activities.

17.

GRANT EXPECTATIONS—MULTIPLICATION OF THE GIFTS

Dear Fr. Zagloba,

NO, I HAVEN'T FORGOTTEN that the roof of the Church needs to be replaced. Now that we have replaced the furnace, it's our number one priority. I've been giving this a little thought.

I think I've told you that taking care of deferred maintenance doesn't qualify as a capital campaign, even if it is a big investment in the parish's buildings. Capital campaigns are typically for new construction, new facilities that capture the imagination and get people excited. We're going to have to try something different.

GRANT EXPECTATIONS

I talked to the Director of Development for the diocese, and he told me about the Catholic Extension Society (CES). They are a pretty neat organization. They do fundraising nationally, and maybe even internationally, and then offer that money in the form of grants to parishes in mission dioceses where it's difficult to raise funds.

Their strategy is brilliant. A parish can submit a grant to them, laying out the need for funds and the timeline for accomplishing the project. Catholic Extension Society will potentially approve a matching gift to the parish. They'll award some amount like $10–15,000, on the condition that the parish raises a similar amount by an agreed upon deadline.

Since our diocese fits the "mission" description, we can potentially apply for a grant that we can use to put up a new roof.

MULTIPLYING LOAVES AND FISHES

Using this kind of matching funds really does help encourage additional gifts. While it's not miraculously multiplying the loaves and the fishes, it does take advantage of the fact that people love a bargain. Research has confirmed that people get a kind of high when they think they're getting a really great deal. My wife tells me that the high is so potent that she has to watch herself at department stores.

A matching gift sets up the expectation that your gift of $1 produces a net result of $2 for the parish. We use this multiplication principal at the Food Bank all the time, and it is essential to our success. For every $1 donated, the Food Bank can provide $9 worth of food to the hungry. People love that their gift makes such a huge impact.

DEADLINES ARE IMPORTANT

The other thing that CES helps to do is create urgency behind the campaign. The roof has been sitting on the church slowly decaying for decades. Hard to make a case for urgency. But if we need to raise $20,000 by Christmas to get another $10,000, we suddenly have a ticking clock to help encourage people to give.

One of the biggest obstacles faced by fundraisers is procrastination. People love your cause, want to donate to your cause, and they'll do it when they have a free moment to take care of it. Except they forget until you remind them again. And then they forget again. Why do you think that advertisers spend so much money putting their message in front of potential customers over and over and over again? Convincing people to ACT NOW is difficult.

God willing, CES approves our request for a matching grant, and then we'll be able to set a timeline that says, "Make your donations by this date." As you saw with replacing the furnace, an urgent need for funds makes a huge impact on the success of the campaign.

ONLINE OPTIONS

We will also need to figure out how to integrate the online giving capability that we're setting to support the campaign. Carmen said that the vendor that we'll be using allows us to create a "Roof Fund" option for donors to select. Tracking donations will be important because CES requires that we show that matching funds are earmarked for the roof.

The other thing that creating the online giving option will allow us to do is encourage monthly giving to support this project. A person might not be able to make a one-time gift of $600 to the roof fund, but they might be willing to do a monthly gift of $50 for a year in addition to their current giving. We just need to be sure to encourage this giving approach when we're talking about it.

REBUILDING THE TEMPLE

Given the results of your emergency fundraising appeal to replace the furnace, I suspect that raising funds for a new roof might not be as hard as we imagine. Remember the life of King Hezekiah in the Old Testament. After a series of faithless kings, he came in with a zeal for restoring the Temple of God and the sacrifices. God inspired him with a zeal to lead the charge and inspired his people to respond generously to their king's request. (2 Chronicles 29–32)

Remember that we're not just putting a roof on an old building. We're on a mission from God. This building is consecrated to His worship, a house of prayer for all the nations (or at least for everyone who visits our city). God will bless our efforts and supernaturally empower us to complete the work.

Blessings,
The Almoner

18.

THOU SHALT SEE THY DONOR FACE TO FACE!

Dear Mrs. Sanderson,

I'M VERY SORRY TO HEAR that you didn't raise as much money as you expected from announcing the food pantry last Sunday. Don't be discouraged. These gifts are only the beginning. You now have four people who have promised to donate every month. That's $150 per month that you didn't have before.

Not only that, now the whole parish is aware of what you're doing, and they know that Fr. Zagloba has given you his blessing. This is a very big deal. Now we move into a new phase of support raising.

MAKING IT PERSONAL

It's easy for someone sitting in a crowd to say to themselves, "Wow, that sounds like a great idea … for someone else." It's the whole phenomenon where a crowd of people will stand around watching a terrible crime happen without doing anything about it. Everyone expects someone else to make the first move.

I think you need to make it more personal. You know pretty much everyone in the parish. Write up a list of 40 people who you know can give $50 a month to the food pantry. If you can think of some people that can easily give $2–300 per month, even better. I want you to try some face-to-face fundraising.

Asking a person face-to-face is perhaps harder on you, but it gives a potential donor the opportunity to consider committing to give. When you're sitting across the coffee table from Mrs. Boynton, she cannot possibly say to herself, "She's asking somebody else to help."

SHARING YOUR STORY AND YOUR PASSION

I want you to think about how excited you were when you first shared this idea with Fr. Zagloba. You are going to share that same zeal and passion with each person you ask. Even if it is a little scary, it's also exciting.

Why do you feel called to serve the hungry at St. Catherine's? Was there some event that triggered your desire? Think about the plans that you've made and the preparations that are already underway.

Prepare a basic script for yourself that hits those main points. Then, pick up your phone and set up an appointment to sit down with every person on your list to tell them your story. You're going to help them to see the big picture of why feeding the hungry is important to you, why it's important to St. Catherine's, and why it should be important to them.

Then ask them, "Would you be in the position to support the food pantry with a gift of $50 (or $100 or $200) per month?" Then be silent. For as long as it takes. Give them the room to think about what you've told them. Weigh the decision. Don't try to rush them, and don't get nervous in the silence. Just pray, "Lord, thy will be done." And wait for them to answer.

The comforting thing is that there are only three possible answers: "Yes," after which you can rejoice and say thank you; "Let me think about it," after which you thank them and set up a time to call them back and get their answer; and "No."

WHAT TO DO WITH A 'NO.'

"No's" are a part of the process. NO! See that didn't hurt a bit. You will hear "no." Probably more than once. There are a couple of different ways to respond to no.

If the person seems offended that you asked them, apologize and thank them for their time. Your relationship with them is more important than their donation. They really shouldn't be surprised when you ask because you should have mentioned your reason for your visit when you called to set up the meeting. Make sure that the phrase, "I want to talk to you about supporting our new food pantry" is in your phone script.

Most people say no for a reason, and you can follow-up with questions that help to bring that reason to light. For instance, if you asked for $200, and their budget just won't stretch that much, that's very reasonable. You might ask them if a lower level commitment would work better. It might not be the right time of the year, or they might have had some unexpected expenses pop up. Perhaps it would be ok for you to talk to them again later in the year.

If the follow-up conversation yields a hard no, thank them for their time and invite them to consider volunteering at the pantry.

MAKE DONATIONS EASY

I'll talk to Fr. Zagloba about including a 'Food Pantry' designation to the online giving options. The best way for people to give is to do it automatically through a monthly credit card or bank transaction. That way they don't have to try to remember to send a check every month, AND you aren't responsible for tracking anyone down if they have forgotten.

Raising money this way will take time and effort on your part, but I think it will pay off in the long run. I'll be praying for you.

Blessings,
The Almoner

P.S. Using a donor tracker will make your job easier. Write the 40 names on a piece of paper. Next to their names, write the date of your phone call, the date of your meeting, their response to your request for support, and how much they have committed to giving. It will make your job easier by keeping all your information in one place. You can also do this on your computer, if you'd like. As time passes, you'll need that information so you can follow up with people who have not paid their pledges. Some people will forget, so you'll want to keep tabs on it.

19.

ENDOWMENTS—THE FUNDRAISER'S APPLE SEED

Dear Fr. Zagloba,

I'VE BEEN TALKING TO the Director of Development for the Diocese, and we've come up with a brilliant idea. An endowment!!!

Stay with me here. You have probably heard in one of your clergy meetings that about 15 years ago, the Bishop created a diocesan Catholic Foundation. This foundation is a separate non-profit from the diocese, and it exists for the sole purpose of shepherding and safeguarding endowment funds for parishes and Catholic organizations in the diocese.

PLANNING FOR ETERNITY

With most giving in the parish, donated funds quickly move to serve some purpose: running a program, fixing toilets, even building a new building. Donors expect to have an immediate impact, and that expectation hopefully bears fruit.

Endowments, on the other hand, provide a way to make a gift that keeps on giving. The endowment prudently invests gifts in building what is called a "corpus." The corpus is the current value of all the gifts ever made to the endowment. We never spend the corpus. A portion of the revenue earned by the corpus can then be spent supporting the parish. The endowment becomes a growing body of income producing assets that can support the parish as long as civilization continues.

Donors, especially donors who can make larger gifts, love being able to make this kind of gift. They know that their gift will continue to bear fruit long after they are gone. They see it as a way to leave a legacy of their support for the Church.

HOW LONG IS FOREVER?

The oldest endowment that I know about is the gift that founded University College at Oxford in England. Back in 1249, a nobleman named William of Dunham willed 310 marks, a huge sum of money at the time, to be invested and support scholars at the college. He wanted to make a gift that would continue to serve the school for future generations. Nearly 800 years later, the Oxford endowment is still going strong.

The long view allows us to start small. If we form an endowment now, it might be 5–10 years before it starts producing meaningful income for the parish. Most gifts will come from people's wills. Besides set up and telling people about it, the process is relatively painless in the short-term. Where it begins to pay off is in the long-term.

Will the Catholic Church exist in 50 years? 100? 500? With the last 2,000 years as a guide, I'd be willing to bet that it will weather any storm that the world or the devil will throw at it. Christ Himself told us that the gates of hell will not prevail against the Church that He founded (Matthew 16:18). So long as the literal "end of the world" doesn't happen, this endowment will continue to have a purpose in 100, 200, or even 500 years.

IMPORTANT, BUT NOT URGENT

The one challenge that we'll face while putting the endowment together is the fact that there will always be something more pressing and more urgent for us to do. If you want an apple right now, you don't plant an apple tree. You go to the store. Planting an orchard takes forethought, a willingness to invest your energy now for something you'll get to enjoy only much later.

My question for you is, "Are you a planter or a grocery shopper?" Realistically, we are both, and ultimately our short game and our long game will work together. I think that our parishioners will appreciate that you're taking steps to ensure the future stability of the parish, especially if we put it in the context of meeting the parish's current needs as well.

Let me know what you think, and we can get started.

Blessings,
The Almoner

20.

ASKING FOR MORE THAN LOOSE CHANGE

Dear Fr. Zagloba,

SOMETHING YOU SAID caught my attention during announcements at Mass. You pointed out Mr. Jenson standing in the back, selling tootsie rolls. Everyone chuckled a little at your joke about cleaning out your couch cushions to find loose change. But I think we need to address if this kind of fundraising has a place in the parish.

IMPULSE CHARITY

Grocery stores are masters of the impulse buy. How many times do you throw a Snickers bar on top of your groceries when you're checking out? The checkout counter is invariable surrounded by racks of items that you did not come to the store to buy: candy, Altoids, stupid magazines, soft drinks. Why? Marketers know that a significant percentage of the people in line will throw one of those things into the basket.

Impulse buys are not the result of conscious thought. You see the candy bar, think "OOOHHHH delicious" and grab one. I've done it myself countless times. I've even had the thought, "I don't need a Snickers," before picking one up and tossing it on top of the diapers.

When Mr. Jenson is standing in the back shaking his bucket and displaying his Tootsie Rolls, he's hitting that same 'impulse' button with the genuinely good intention of raising money for our seminarians. People give automatically, almost without thinking, just like with the Snickers. They might have a vague idea of wanting to help, or they might give because they like Mr. Jenson.

Or, they might give because the person in front of them gave and they feel guilty about not following suit.

WE LOSE WHEN WE LOWER THE BAR

Why do I bring this up? Obviously, Mr. Jenson did sell some candy, so it is working to a degree. The problem with impulse fundraising is that it dramatically limits how much money you can raise. Think about it. The grocery store does not put high dollar items next to the checkout line. Everything is cheap. It's like there's an unwritten rule about what the average person will spend without thinking.

The same principle works for impulse charity. A person might give the change in their pocket or pull out a fiver. Maybe even a twenty if he's also in the Knights of Columbus. But you won't get any serious, high-level gifts. Nobody walks out of our church with $100 worth of Tootsie rolls. Any approach that relies on impulse charity is going to raise a small amount of money. Simple math works against it.

BIGGER GIFTS, BIGGER IMPACT

If we as a church want to financially support our seminarians, it only makes sense to do it the most effective way possible. And this means giving people the opportunity to make a well-considered, thoughtful, and generous gift. I know it will mean more work. But the results will be vastly larger if you are asking people to give larger gifts.

If you ask 100 people to give you $1, the maximum that you'll get is $100. The likelihood is that you'll get far less. If on the other hand, you ask 100 people to give you $100, you might get only get three or four people who decide to give at that level—and bring in $300–400. The reduced number of gifts still brings in 3–4 times as much money because you set your sights higher.

The difference between the pocket-change impulse gift and the intentional large gift is that the person doing the 'ask' is more intentional. Mr. Jenson does very little besides standing in the back with two little buckets filled with Tootsie Rolls and loose change. To start getting larger gifts, he'll have to give people a reason why they should give bigger gifts. That might include bringing a seminarian to share his testimony about the call to the priesthood. It might mean producing some high-quality materials or using the ones that the diocese has already produced. Most importantly, it will mean sitting down and talking to people one-on-one.

The result of a more intentional fundraising approach is raising a lot more money. It will also increase the level of investment our parish has in the seminarians' success. Giving will create a deeper connection to the activity of the Church in the diocese.

THE RIGHT APPROACH MAKES ALL THE DIFFERENCE

Obviously, Mr. Jenson is trying to do something good, and I applaud him. I just want him to be able to make the biggest difference that he can with his efforts. It might take way more time to raise $500 by nickels and dimes than it does to raise $5,000 by asking the right person once. I know that he can do better.

Of course, you as the pastor need to allow him to do so. We're about to try to raise the money to re-roof the Church, so you might not want him doing a more intensive fundraising drive. In fact, his willingness to stand out in the back with his buckets might be a good indication that he has the right stuff to be on the roof committee. He has already shown his interest in raising money. Maybe it's time to put that drive to work.

Blessings,
The Almoner

P.S. I do realize that the Salvation Army does impulse fundraising every Christmas ringing their little bells outside Walmart. It works because they are doing it with something like 50,000 volunteers at 3,000 stores for over a month. Impulse fundraising at that scale can work. Loose change from 100,000,000 people does eventually add up to real money. It's a different story when the audience is the same 500 people you see every week. You can only sell so many Tootsie Rolls.

21.

TIME, TALENT, TITHE =
A LIFE OF PRAYER, SERVICE, AND THANKSGIVING

Dear Fr. Zagloba,

I'VE BEEN WORKING on the plan for the Annual Stewardship Campaign that we've discussed. Since this is our first year, I think we should keep it simple. We can add more elements in future years but doing it well this year will open the door for us improve it in the future.

I suggest that we hold it over three weekends: one focusing on "Time," one on "Talent," and the last on "Tithe." During each weekend, you'll preach on that weekend's focus using the scriptures of the day. Hopefully, you won't have to stretch it too much. Then at the end of Mass, we'll have a speaker talk about the same topic, but using their testimony. On the third weekend, we'll put the pledge cards and pencils in the pew and ask everyone to commit for the upcoming year. We should encourage everyone to sign up online to make monthly recurring gifts.

FIRST THINGS FIRST

When we talk about "Time," we should focus on prayer. Specifically, intercessory prayer for the parish and the people in the parish. Putting this on the first weekend is extremely important. We need to point to the fact—THE FACT—that the most powerful thing anyone can do for our Church is to pray for it.

It's the kind of thing that is so obvious that you might not realize it unless someone points it out. It is basic. No one can do anything that will be more effective or have bigger results than asking God to do something for the parish.

We should suggest that they think about what in our parish life is most important to them: evangelical outreach, ministry to the poor, youth ministry, elder care, liturgy, music—whatever it might be. And then we will ask them to commit to pray with that focus for the next year on a regular (daily) basis.

Everyone can do it, from the oldest to the youngest. Doesn't cost anything. You don't need any specific skills. And in a years' time, God will start answering prayers. People will be amazed!

How do I know this? One of the privileges of serving the poor is that I get to see God move in response to my prayers. Did you know that the biggest grants that I've gotten came from incoming calls? I pray and ask God to help me find the money that the food bank needs to feed the hungry, and I get phone calls out of the blue inviting me to submit a grant application. Over and over. For hundreds of thousands of dollars! And often just in the nick of time. The Lord has provided money for trucks, warehouses, forklifts, staff members, you name it. I prayed for something specific, God opened the door for me to write a grant, and before you know it there was a check in the mail. Prayer is not just some empty pious practice for little old ladies. Prayer stirs the action of Almighty God, who holds all things in being simply because He so desires.

Highlighting prayer at the beginning of our Annual Stewardship Campaign will help people understand that we aren't just doing another fundraiser. We want to help our people to live the Gospel more fully.

GET PEOPLE INVOLVED

The second week will focus on "Talents," the abilities that people have that can be used for the good of the Church and the world. Every gift and talent that we have finds its most perfect fulfillment and highest purpose when we put it at God's disposal. A singer's vocal talent can find no greater expression than in worship. A carpenter's handiwork has no greater destiny than to beautify the House of God. A love of serving has no better outlet than ministering to the needs of others in the name of Jesus.

We should plan to do our ministry fair during this weekend and ask people to find a new way to get involved. We can even direct them to ministries outside of our four walls. I know we have a team of people who serve at the soup kitchen on a regular basis. I bet they could use some extra hands. If people don't find a ministry in the parish that excites them, we should encourage them to look at some of the other parishes around town. If they still can't find a good match, maybe that means they need to start something new.

Now, I know that not everybody is going to jump up and say, "YES! I need another extracurricular activity!" But getting involved is a great way to build relationships and feel more connected to the rest of the community. Let's face it. You just don't get to know somebody very well if the only time you see them is sitting next to them in a pew for an hour each Sunday. It helps to get your hands dirty working on a project together.

THE CONVERSION OF THE WALLET

The third weekend will focus on "Tithe." You'll notice that I am not using the word treasure, which is the standard slogan for stewardship campaigns. I don't think that money is a treasure. It's just stuff that moths eat, rust decays, and thieves steal (Matthew 6:19). Money buys more stuff, most of which ends up in the garbage can. When you use the word *treasure* connected with money, it evokes the wrong kind of response in people. It suggests that they should hide it away and keep it safe from grasping hands.

Jesus told the rich young man to give all his stuff away (Mark 10:17–22). Only then would he have TREASURE ... stored up in the vaults of Heaven, where it will last eternally. When we talk *treasure,* this is the kind we want coming to mind.

Tithes are different. A tithe is a thanksgiving offering. It is a gift that you give to God to say "thank you" for all the things that He has given us. And God makes promises to those who tithe. In the book of Malachi, God challenges His people to begin to bring their tithes and offerings into the temple.

Bring the whole tithe into the storehouse, that there may be food in my house. Put me to the test, says the LORD of hosts, and see if I do not open the floodgates of heaven for you, and pour down upon you blessing without measure! I will rebuke the locust for you so that it will not destroy your crops, and the vine in the field will not be barren, says the LORD of hosts. All the nations will call you blessed, for you will be a delightful land, says the LORD of hosts. (Malachi 3:10–12)

The speaker for the third weekend should already be tithing—I know that there must be a few in the parish. We'll find them by looking at our donor record. They'll be obvious. Anybody who tithes does so for a reason. It pinches the budget. The speaker needs to talk about their reasons for tithing. They should speak about how God moved them to give the full 10 percent, and how He's blessed them in response to their joyful generosity. The speaker should thank everyone who is already tithing, encourage everyone who is giving at a lower level to consider increasing their monthly gift and gently challenge those who are not giving to commit to give something. Remember that a small gift out of someone's poverty is more pleasing to God than a large gift out of someone's surplus.

WHERE YOUR TREASURE IS, THERE WILL YOUR HEART BE ALSO

I can tell what's important to you by looking at two things ... your checkbook and your calendar. You invest your money and your time into things you value. The whole point of this stewardship campaign is to help people look at their checkbooks and calendars for a moment of self-examination, of self-discovery. Even more importantly, a moment of conversion.

If more of our people can live a life of prayer, service, and generosity, we will transform our parish. I can't tell you how excited this makes me.

Blessings,
The Almoner

P.S. One other thing I like about changing our slogan to 'Time, Talent, and Tithe' is that it isn't a cliché. They're so used to hearing "Time, Talent, and Treasure," that their brains shut down the moment they hear it.

Also, remember that tithing is virtuous and pleasing to God. You should feel confident when you're preaching about tithing because you're asking them to do something good!

22.

GO THEREFORE AND MAKE ... STEWARDS? NO! DISCIPLES!

Dear Fr. Zagloba,

I UNDERSTAND WHY you don't want to jump into a full-blown annual stewardship campaign right now. Your concern that the focus on committing to pray, serve, and give might be too much for the parish is certainly valid.

Let's back up for a minute. First off, we don't have to jump into campaign mode right away. You're the pastor of the parish, and you've got to keep the pastoral perspective in mind. Let's take a moment to look at how stewardship fits into the big picture.

WHAT'S THE BIG PICTURE?

When the bishops wrote the pastoral letter, "Stewardship: A Disciple's Response," the title itself is a crucial clue to understanding the big picture. Stewardship is something that a disciple does. It's the lifestyle that a disciple lives. It's the way disciples view and use their time, talents, and material resources.

Before we ever get to stewardship, we start with discipleship. Discipleship is the process by which the Church teaches people to live the life of faith. Jesus said in the great commission, "Go, therefore, and make disciples, baptizing them in the name of the Father, Son, and the Holy Spirit, teaching them to observe all that I have commanded you" (Matthew 28:19). The work of the Apostles, and your work—by extension and ordination—is to make disciples.

What does it mean to make disciples? Many have written about the topic, but the Catechism of the Catholic Church sums it up pretty neatly:

Becoming a disciple of Jesus means accepting the invitation to belong to God's family, to live in conformity with His way of life: "For whoever does the will of my Father in heaven is my brother, and sister, and mother." (Paragraph 2233)

STEWARDSHIP IS NOT OPTIONAL

Making disciples means teaching people how to live their lives according to the will of the Father. Stewardship is a part of that. The model that Jesus gave us to live as disciples is the good and faithful steward. The one who puts his talents to work in the marketplace and can give his master ten talents upon his return (Matthew 25:14–30).

The parable of the steward also points out that the life of stewardship is not some 'optional thing' that Christians can do if we can get around to it. The Lord banished the servant who buried his talent to the outer darkness. Refusing to embrace the model of the good steward will have dire consequences!

If stewardship is not optional for the disciple, then teaching about stewardship is not optional for the disciple-maker. This means you, Fr. Zagloba, with all due respect. You have a responsibility to teach the members of our parish to live the Gospel generously.

And you're right … preaching and teaching about stewardship might shake people up a bit. It might irritate them because it will force them to look at their lives and realize that they need to make some considerable changes. People might even get angry with you because they are comfortable the way they are and you're messing everything up.

But! But! They might also be converted.

BECOME A CHILD OF GOD

"For whoever does the will of my Father in heaven is my brother, and sister, and mother"(Matthew 12:50). What an amazing promise!!! To be a part of God's family is nothing less than the kingdom of God itself, a gift from God to all who live their lives according to the Father's will. Entering Gods' kingdom is what stewardship is all about.

You want the people in our parish to live as sons and daughters of the Most High God! You'll be teaching them how when you help them to fully embrace the call to be disciples of Jesus Christ and live a life of stewardship. You could never give a greater gift to anyone. The gift passes through the Cross and leads to a life of eternal rejoicing in the presence of Most Holy Trinity!

I hope this gets you as excited as it gets me. Perhaps, because of my days as an atheist and my dramatic conversion, this seems like the most awesome thing that could happen to a person. Or maybe it's bigger than my own experience and is, in fact, the most awesome possible thing that could happen to any person who has ever lived. I'm inclined to think the latter.

Pray about it and let me know if you want to move forward with the stewardship campaign. We can think of other ways to approach the topic of stewardship if now isn't the right time. But you don't get to bypass the topic altogether … it's just part of what you are called to do.

Blessings,
The Almoner

P.S. The best first step in this may be to start praying and fasting for the Lord to give you a vision for how He wants you to 'make disciples.' I think stewardship campaign, but I could be wrong. Jesus not only knows the way, He IS the way.

23.

BUILD AN ARMY OF VOLUNTEER FUNDRAISERS

Dear Mrs. Sanderson,

I'M SO SORRY to hear that you're feeling discouraged. I completely understand the feeling of "I just can't do this." I went through a season as a fundraiser when I was supposed to do door-to-door cold calls to businesses for donations. I simply couldn't force myself to do it. It was like running into a brick wall. It just wasn't my style. Face-to-face fundraising might not be your gift! Don't worry: all hope is not lost.

YOU NEED REINFORCEMENTS!

The Battle belongs to the Lord! Right now, you're feeling beaten, discouraged, like an army that is being chased away by the enemy. Fundraising for the new food pantry is conquering you, to the point that you are ready to wave the white flag of surrender. Don't despair!!!

You have a passion for serving the poor and a vision for making the new food pantry warm and welcoming. You are irreplaceable! You just need help with fundraising. We need to find someone who shares your vision but has no problem talking to people and asking them for money.

My first thought is Mr. Jenson. I laugh as I think of him. He knows everyone in the parish and has a heart of gold. I think he sold over 1,000 Tootsie Rolls this year, which must be some kind of record. I know I took home more than my fair share. Let's try to set up a lunch with him so you can tell him the idea of the food pantry, and I can explain the fundraising method that we want to use.

We can start by asking him to use the process that I described to you in my last letter. Person-to-person fundraising is still your best bet. He can use the list of people who you created as his starting point and add his own contacts if we need to go further.

If he looks at the list and says that it seems like it's too much work, we can ask him to help find some more volunteer solicitors. In volunteer 'terminology' he'll be the 'fundraising captain.' He's a veteran, so I think he'll like that. He can build a team of volunteer fundraisers to make sure everyone on your list gets a personal invitation to support the food pantry.

FORCE MULTIPLIER

There's no shame in admitting that you can't do everything in this new ministry. The fact that fundraising ties a knot in your stomach doesn't mean that you're not supposed to persist in starting this food pantry. St. Paul tells us to think of ourselves as parts of the Body of Christ and possessing different gifts. Just because you're a hand doesn't mean that you should feel ashamed that you're not an elbow. You just need someone like Mr. Jenson to be the elbow that helps you to reach out to others.

In military terms, a force multiplier is something that enables a person or unit to have a bigger impact that they would have without it. So, for instance, a cannon enables a soldier to make a bigger dent in the enemy walls than a sling shot. Bringing in volunteers to help will enable you to do things that you never could by yourself.

You're not going to be able to do all the work that this pantry requires, but you do have the vision to be the leader. A big part of the success of this ministry is understanding how many volunteers you're going to need and what they will be doing. As you enlist new people to serve with their gifts, your ability to accomplish your goals will increase exponentially. With the right team of volunteers, you'll be able to do things that you never thought possible.

GATHERING THE TROOPS

So, start thinking about what kind of help you'll need for the pantry. We've already identified fundraising as a place to start. What about people to help you to pick up the food from the food bank? You'll need some strong backs for that. Sorting the food into boxes for distribution? That's just time-consuming, so maybe the youth group could help there. What about people talking to the folks who come in for help? You said you want this to be more than just a food giveaway. You want to find out what's going on in people's lives and find more ways to help them. Getting helpers with the right kind of attitude and personality will make that vision a reality.

Your role as a leader is bringing all the different people together and giving them the vision of what's supposed to happen and how they're going to do it. Just like your list of potential donors, you'll need to come up with a list of potential volunteers. Your list will have two columns—the first column will list the different volunteer roles you need to fill. The second column will be the list of folks that have the gifts to fill in that role.

When you start making phone calls, you don't have to go so far as to get a hard, long-term commitment. What you're looking for is a "Yes, give me a call when you need a hand." You're creating a list of volunteers that you can call on in your time of need. People will give freely of their time, but they won't be able to do it all the time. So, you'll need two or three people who are available for each slot. Having some backup people also helps prevent burn out. And don't worry, most people find that asking for volunteers is MUCH easier than asking for donations.

SOLDIER ON!

Please don't be discouraged! This setback is an opportunity for you to get more people involved in your ministry. In the end, finding the right people to serve beside you, will make the difference between victory and defeat.

Blessings,
The Almoner

P.S. We can also put a list of volunteer needs in the bulletin once you've got your list. That will bring in volunteers that you might not have thought to call. A benefit of soliciting volunteers this way is that anyone who calls in after reading the bulletin announcement is interested in helping. In fact, you can reach out to people this way first, and then make phone calls to fill in any gaps. Easy-peasy!

24.

ENTITLEMENTS ARE CHARITY WITHOUT CHARITY

Dear Mrs. Sanderson,

I WOULDN'T BE upset with Mr. Jenson. He asked an important question. I am sorry that I didn't prepare you to answer it, but I'll talk to him myself if you'd like. I don't think he completely shut down the possibility of getting involved … he just wants to understand why you're doing what you're doing.

To sum up his question, he asked, "Why are we setting up a food pantry when the people we want to serve can get food stamps?" He doesn't realize it, but he points right at the heart of the difference between "entitlement" and "charity."

LOVE IS THE KEY

The difference between a food stamp's card and the food pantry you want to start is kind of like the difference between getting a meal at fast food restaurant and eating Sunday dinner at Grandma's house. Sure, they might serve the same food (although Grandma's brownies will beat the stuffing out of fast food any old day), but it's the intangible thing that makes the biggest difference. It's the love.

When people come to our food pantry, we want them to experience all the love that you shower on your grandchildren. Mr. Jenson asked, "What if they just keep coming back?" GREAT!!! That gives you an opportunity to build a relationship with them. Perhaps look a little more deeply into their problems. And let the love they experience at your food pantry take root and bear fruit.

Most people who will come to our food pantry are in a heap of trouble. They might have medical problems, drug and alcohol addictions, and certainly financial problems. No one is excited about going to a food pantry to get help. It's almost always a last resort.

THE PIT OF DESPAIR

I hope you don't mind, but I want to share a personal story. Would it surprise you to learn that I was homeless during my late twenties? I was living and working in Hollywood when I had a complete nervous breakdown. I lost everything. My fiancé, my house, my job, and maybe worst of all, I lost my mind. The doctor that saw me said I would have to be institutionalized and that I would never work again.

I couldn't think. I couldn't work. I had no insurance, and I couldn't afford medications I needed to keep my brain from spinning off into "la-la" land. How did I survive? Charity. My sister, my old college roommate, and finally my parents brought me into their homes. Social workers call this kind of homelessness "couch-surfing." I was totally dependent on the kindness of others. Without it, I would have stayed that crazy guy that you see walking around downtown in the middle of the night (which I did for more nights than I want to remember).

It was more terrible than I can possibly describe. The only reason I survived, the reason I did not kill myself, is that people loved me and put up with me in my wretched state for a long time. It took me YEARS to fully recover. And I was hard to love.

THE LIGHT OF CHARITY

When I was in that black pit, I was powerless to do anything about my situation. Thankfully, my family and friends jumped in and gave me a couch to sleep on and food to eat. Even in that darkness, they blessed me.

Unfortunately, there are a lot of people out there who don't have anyone. One of the effects of the disintegration of the family is that many people are completely isolated. They have no one to turn to when the darkness threatens to overwhelm them.

And let's face it. Food stamps don't care. They can't. Food stamps and other public assistance were created to provide a small amount of supplemental income to people who meet the specified economic characteristics. It can't comfort the new widow, the single mother, the disabled veteran. Not the way you can.

I hope you realize you're not just handing out food, you're walking with people out of darkness. Loving them in the midst of terrible situations. Serving them with no hope of repayment. Hoping that the light of your charity will have the same transformative effect that it did in my life.

And that's the answer to Mr. Jenson's question. The world can provide bread and circuses to the poor, but it cannot love them. Only love, the self-sacrificing love we see on the Cross, can save them. That is why you're starting a food pantry.

Blessings,
The Almoner

P.S. If Mr. Jenson still isn't interested once he's heard your answer, don't worry. We want someone who is as passionate about your vision for the food pantry as we are. We'll move on and find someone else to help you fundraise.

25.

FUNDRAISING TWO BY TWO, A BIBLICAL BUDDY SYSTEM

Dear Mrs. Sanderson,

THAT'S GREAT NEWS! I hoped that Mr. Jenson would sign on once he understood what you're trying to do. I did NOT expect him to commit to giving $100 per month, but this goes to show you … people will respond when you tell them your mission, your "why."

You now have about $250 worth of monthly support committed and need $1,000. As a word of encouragement, do you realize that your committed support already totals $3,000 per year? Did you ever think you'd be able to raise that much money just by asking people? And we're just getting started.

Now that Mr. Jenson has agreed to help, I want to propose an approach that I think will work. It's called "volunteer solicitation," and you'll use all the work that you've done so far. You're going to work from the list of potential donors that you've already created, and Mr. Jenson will help you knock on the doors. Then you'll meet with the potential donors, but you'll take Mr. Jenson with you.

KNOW YOUR PLAN BUT GO WITH THE FLOW

I understand you're feeling timid about asking a donor one-on-one. That's why you'll take Mr. Jenson with you as your partner. He said he'll make the calls to set up the appointments. Great! Make sure that he sets up a time when it's possible for him to go with you.

Now, this isn't about trying to pressure people into making a gift. Absolutely not. It's about having someone on your team in the room with you, in case your tongue gets stuck to the roof of your mouth. I think you'll find this won't be the case, especially once you get talking about the mission. But just having someone beside you will make all the difference.

It's good to have a basic structure for the meeting in mind, but know that you can break it if you think it's necessary, or if the conversation seems like it's going in an unexpected direction. Use your judgment. Mr. Jenson is an old salesman; he'll know the right moment to transition from small talk to discussing your mission and "the ask."

Start your meeting with small talk. You know these people and have for years. Once you've had a chance to catch up, you'll need to transition to talking about the mission. You could ask Mr. Jenson to say something like, "We think you'll be excited to hear about the food pantry that St. Catherine's is starting." Then you share your passion for serving the poor. Answer any questions that come up, especially those like Mr. Jenson's about why a food pantry at the parish provides something other than what is available through public assistance. Don't be afraid to get excited when you talk about this project. It's contagious.

Once you've shared the mission and answered any questions, Mr. Jenson can then chime in with "the ask." He's probably better at this than I am, but he can say something like, "We hope that you'll be able to make this food pantry a reality. Would you be in the position to consider supporting it with $X per month?" Before you go into the meeting, you and he should pick a number that seems appropriate for the person that you're meeting.

Then you both need to sit quietly and wait for an answer. Seriously, don't say anything. At all. If the silence stretches into minutes, GREAT! That means the person is thinking it over. You'll be tempted to break the silence, but you must resist with all your might.

You know that the person will say either "Yes," "No," or "Maybe" (or some variation like, "I'll think about it.") Just wait for them to pick one. And say a prayer internally, that if God wants this person to give, He will grant them the grace to be generous.

A PLAN WITH A BIBLICAL PEDIGREE

We know this approach works because it is the way God sent Moses and Aaron to tell Pharaoh, "Let my people go!" That's a hard ask. And talk about a hostile audience. You won't face any rejection that severe. Your friends will refuse very politely if they are not able to support the ministry. You're in very little danger of being cast into a dungeon.

Like you, Moses was terrified of going to his meeting with Pharaoh. God sent his brother Aaron along with him to be the spokesman. Just having a teammate made all the difference in the world. If you remember from the story, once they got into the room, Moses did almost all the talking. He just needed a buddy to get him past his anxiety and the fear of speaking publicly.

BUILDING MOMENTUM

I think it took a lot of courage for you to ask Mr. Jenson, AND to go back to him with answers to his questions. You're doing a great job! I think that you'll have all the resources you need to move forward in just a couple of months.

Blessings,
The Almoner

P.S. I think that your newfound passion for serving the poor is a grace from the Lord. Continue to press on in prayer and action, and I do not doubt that you'll succeed. You'll do things you never dreamed possible.

26.

HURRICANES—A TIME FOR TALENTS

Dear Fr. Zagloba,

I'M SITTING AT HOME watching the hurricane winds bend trees almost in half. Rain moving horizontally is quite the sight to see. The Food Bank is closed today, as is most of the state. It's not as bad as we'd feared, thank God, but down in Florida and the islands to the south the damage is terrible to contemplate.

I am glad that you did a second collection at Mass for the hurricane victims. It's important to encourage people to get involved with the recovery even as the storm is beginning to batter us. I want to suggest a few ways to make this call to action more powerful.

ENCOURAGE THOUGHTFUL GIVING

When you announced the second collection, I don't recall that you mentioned where the funds would be going except in the most general way. This is a very important piece of information. Will we be sending the money to Catholic Relief Services, or do you know a parish down there that is in the storm's path? Knowing what their donations will be doing and where they are going will have a significant impact on the level of giving in the parish.

Secondly, a second collection that you haven't advertised in advance falls into the category of "impulse charity." You're only going to get whatever cash people are carrying with them. I rarely carry cash, and I know that I'm not alone. So, if you want to gather a more substantial donation, we should run the collection for several weeks and enable an online giving option.

Sharing a clear plan for the donations and giving people enough time to prayerfully consider making a gift will significantly increase the amount the parish will be able to give to people in storm-ravaged areas.

I also think you should consider going a step further.

TIME TO GET OUR HANDS DIRTY

We should think about putting together a mission team to go down into the storm wrecked areas. Not immediately, because many of the areas are only open to emergency personnel right now. It would be best to partner with another parish that can line up about a week's worth of projects for however many people we can bring down with us. We should plan it with enough warning for us to purchase the supplies that we'll need using donations. The rebuilding process will take months, so there's plenty of time to do this without rushing around like crazy people.

It is not an outlandish idea. I have friends who attend Protestant churches that send mission groups all over the world to build churches, hospitals, schools, and homes. Each missionary is responsible for paying for their trip, and they often raise $3,000 or more per head to go. The mission trips are so popular that they keep a waiting list. They don't have enough slots to take all the people who want to go.

The fact is that people like to do something concrete. They get satisfaction when they look at something they have built that will impact people's lives. And we don't even have to send people to another continent to serve! The need is just a bus trip away, but the experience will be the treasure of a lifetime.

It's so exciting! We can have our laborers share their experiences after Mass when they return. We can put some posters with pictures of the team at work out in the narthex. All this will help the people of the parish feel like they have served alongside the hurricane-relief missionaries, as indeed they have through their giving. Some give by going, and some go by giving.

DISCOVER THE BLESSINGS HIDDEN OUTSIDE OUR COMFORT ZONES

When you're thinking about building a discipleship/stewardship culture at the parish, think about how you're going to invite people to live this kind of life. It's not going to happen by accident. And it's not going to happen without your leadership. Serving people in a hurricane ravaged area is a terrific way for people to *live discipleship.*

Exercising leadership doesn't mean you have to do everything. You can deputize a leader for this mission project and give the authority to make it happen. You're just following the model Jesus gave you. As just one man, He couldn't get everywhere with His proclamation of the kingdom. He selected 12 from among His disciples to be sent forth. His Apostles. Sending out a mission trip to serve in the hurricane's aftermath follows that same model.

Let's face it. You can't go wrong if you're following in the footsteps of the Master. Even if it pushes you out of your comfort zone. Even if it pushes our parish out of its comfort zone. When Jesus asked a bunch of fishermen, tax collectors, and others to become traveling preachers, it was like a hurricane sweeping through their lives. Comfort zones demolished.

The kingdom of God is right over there. Do you see it? Outside our comfort zone.

Blessings,
The Almoner

P.S. If you think that a week is too much, what about a long weekend. We've never done a service trip with the parish. It will get easier with practice. Just don't be afraid to take the first leap.

27.

CASTING A BROADER NET; REQUESTS FOR SUPPORT

Dear Mrs. Sanderson,

I THINK REACHING OUT to local businesses for donations is a great idea. I think you should start by sending out "requests for support."

A "request for support" is a kind of business letter that asks for a specific gift for the food pantry. It is kind of like a grant except that you're not going to be sending it to a formally established grant maker like a private foundation or government agency. They don't need a formal structure like a grant—a simple business letter works just fine. Since the food pantry is a ministry of the Church, we don't need to send proof of our non-profit status. Sending it on Church letterhead should be sufficient, though you should mention that the donation will be tax-deductible.

FISHING FOR DONATIONS

Requests for support typically ask for in-kind donations—equipment or products rather than funds. The cost to a business of an in-kind donation is less than for cash donation because they are only donating the wholesale value of the item requested.

We can request equipment or food with this kind of solicitation. For instance, we can write to Lowe's and ask them for a refrigerator to keep perishable food cold. Or racking to store food. Send me your list of necessary equipment, and we'll figure out a matched list of businesses to ask for each item. We might also reach out to our Saturday Farmer's Market and ask if we can pick up what's left over at the end of the day.

To get the best possible success from this effort, we'll need to plant some seeds ahead of time. Talk to Mr. Jenson and let him know that we're going to send him out 'visiting.' Once we have a list of business names that we're going to contact, we'll send him around to introduce himself and our mission. His job will be to make a good impression (something he does very easily) and get the name of the person who can make decisions at the store. The store manager at a big chain or the business owner at a local business usually has the authority to approve your request.

When we're preparing the list, we'll want to look to see if the businesses have websites and if their websites have a "community relations" section. Many of the bigger ones do. Companies will often tell you what kinds of ministries they will or won't support. Feeding people falls under "basic needs" and is well received, but some businesses like to focus on things like education, job skills, etc. That's their prerogative, so we should focus our attention on asking businesses that like to support what we're going to be doing. Some bigger businesses will have a formal grant application process, which we'll need to skip for now. Grants tend to go to organizations that have a history of at least a few years.

GIVE YOUR STORY A HOOK

Once Mr. Jenson gets us the name of the person we'll be sending our letter, we can tailor a letter like this to request the equipment that we're looking to get:

Dear (Insert name),

While most of the city seems to be thriving and growing, on the South side of town, life is a little bleaker. Crime rates and drug issues have pushed out many of the businesses, making it difficult for many of the locals to find good jobs. It's hard to believe, but many people struggle just to get enough food to eat.

Over the past couple of years, St. Catherine's Catholic Church has seen a dramatic increase in the number of people coming to ask for help. Dozens of families visit every week, just looking for enough food to get by. For this reason, St. Catherine's is starting a food pantry to meet their needs. The goal is to provide for their basic human needs while also helping them to get back on their feet. Sometimes a little bit of help and some compassion can make all the difference.

We need your help to make our new food pantry a reality. Would you please consider donating a Frigidaire 18 Cu. Ft. Freezer Refrigerator to store frozen and perishable food items that we will give to people in need? Frozen meat and vegetables and fresh produce are some of the healthiest items that we can provide, but without the right kind of storage, we won't be able to offer these to our neighbors.

A new refrigerator-freezer would make a tremendous impact in the lives of people in our community who are struggling to get enough food. We expect that we'll be able to serve 50–100 families per month right off the bat, and we expect that to grow. The food pantry is a ministry of St. Catherine's Catholic Church, a tax-exempt organization, so your donation will be tax-deductible.

Please let me know if you need any additional information. My email is (email), and my phone number is (phone number). Please feel free to call me if you have any questions.

Thank you so much for your time and consideration.

Blessings,

Norma Sanderson

You see the basic structure: explain the need, tell what we're doing to meet the need, explain how the business can help. We can adjust the letter to reflect the different equipment that we'll be requesting.

THE ONE THAT GOT AWAY

One thing that I want to warn you of with this approach. Some of the people that we ask will say "no." Most of them will say "no." That's ok. We just need to plan to ask enough people to get to some "yeses."

If you haven't figured this out yet, one of the core virtues you need for fundraising is humility. You need the courage to get up and dust yourself off after a "no" and ask someone else. Or even ask the same person again.

Not that I think you'll lose heart after your first "no." I've already seen how determined you are to make this work. Be encouraged. We'll be celebrating our first success sooner than you think.

Blessings,
The Almoner

P.S. If my letter doesn't sound exactly the way you want, feel free to make some changes. Or you might ask Mr. Jenson to send it out after he's met with people. The better connection we have with a PERSON in the business, the better our chances of bringing in a donation.

Also, let's see if Fr. Zagloba will put the list of equipment we need in the church bulletin. It only makes sense to ask the people who are closest to the ministry.

28.

THE WIDOW'S MIGHT; THE POWER OF GIVING

Dear Fr. Zagloba,

I'VE BEEN THINKING ABOUT what you said about the dangers of sounding like a prosperity gospel preacher. The image of a televangelist comes to mind, mopping his brow with a white handkerchief and talking about how Jesus wants you to live your best life now. How prayer will help you get the big house you want, the fast car you want, and the job you want. "If you just give to my church, God will answer your prayers." Taking that promise and the scripture that backs it up straight to the bank with a multimillion dollar home and a private jet. Danger, it's a trap!

That's certainly not the model you want to follow. A bible story came to mind.

> He sat down opposite the treasury and observed how the crowd put money into the treasury. Many rich people put in large sums. A poor widow also came and put in two small coins worth a few cents. Calling his disciples to himself, he said to them, "Amen, I say to you, this poor widow put in more than all the other contributors to the treasury. For they have all contributed from their surplus wealth, but she, from her poverty, has contributed all she had, her whole livelihood." (Mark 12:41–44)

My son got a beautiful picture Bible for Christmas this year. I've read the entire thing cover to cover at least twice now. When we got to this story, the picture affected me so powerfully that I started crying. Try explaining that to a four-year-old. The picture showed a young widow, face creased with grief, holding a child no older than my son. It shook me.

I've always pictured the widow as a woman at the end of her life, but the image fleshed out the story in an unexpected way ... A young woman just lost her husband, and now has no way to support her beloved child. She takes her offering to the Temple as if saying, "God, you have to DO something! Help Me! I cannot do this without You!" An act of giving, yes, but more importantly an act of faith. One that pleased Jesus so much that the Evangelists recorded it for us to ponder 2,000 years later.

THE MEASURE WITH WHICH WE MEASURE SHALL BE MEASURED OUT TO US ...

At the Food Bank, we get lots of donations. One stands out in my mind because it has the same quality we see in the story of the widow. One envelope contained a $5 bill and a hand-written note. The donor wrote that he was out of work and just about out of money. He donated and asked us to pray that he would find a job.

What's amazing is that in this case, we heard the rest of the story. The person wrote a few weeks later to thank us for the prayers and let us know that he had gotten a new job out the blue. He thanked us for our prayers and praised the Lord that He had smiled upon his offering

Now it's certainly easy enough to say that you can't make a direct connection between the donation and getting a new job. Especially if you have the bias that says that God doesn't exist, or that He's some distant watchmaker who never interferes in the lives of regular people. But this is not our faith. Our faith tells us that God hears the cry of the poor. "This poor one cried out and the LORD heard, and from all his distress he saved him" (Psalm 34:7). His loving kindness is from generation to generation. Jesus teaches, "Blessed are you who are poor, for the kingdom of God is yours" (Luke 6:20).

THE DANGER OF "PROSPERITY" THEOLOGY

Now the danger in this is that there are wolves in sheep's clothing that run around telling poor people, "Jesus wants you to live your best life now. If you give today, then you'll get that new job, that fancy car, that big house." Meanwhile, the wolves live high on the hog off those donations in big houses, with fancy cars, and even airplanes in some cases. Let's face it; it was one of the major criticisms during the Protestant Reformation. Fattened shepherds with emaciated flocks cause terrible scandal in the Church and the world. Always have, always will. Just a few years ago, a German bishop was suspended by the Pope for building a $40 million residence for himself. And we wonder why the number of practicing Catholics in Germany has fallen off a cliff?

But this doesn't take away from the truth of our faith that God does hear the cry of the poor and that the offering of the poor man is exceedingly pleasing to Him. God sees and, more importantly, He responds to our offerings, especially to the offerings to the poor. He taught us to ask for our daily bread. He means that He is prepared to give us daily bread. Not figuratively. Not merely 'spiritual bread' (although this is also included). Real, sink-your-teeth-into, fill-your-belly daily bread.

If you think I'm off base, go back to the Israelites. God provided them with daily bread. Has God changed? Has His willingness to feed His sheep vanished? Jesus said, "I am the gate. Whoever enters through me will be saved and will come in and go out and find pasture" (John 10:9). Pasture means food!

Or even better, look at the encounter between the Prophet Elijah and the widow at Zarephath.

> When he arrived at the entrance of the city, a widow was there gathering sticks; he called out to her, "Please bring me a small cupful of water to drink." She left to get it, and he called out after her, "Please bring along a crust of bread." She said, "As the Lord, your God, lives, I have nothing baked; there is only a handful of flour in my jar and a little oil in my jug. Just now I was collecting a few sticks, to go in and prepare something for myself and my son; when we have eaten it, we shall die." Elijah said to her, "Do not be afraid. Go and do as you have said. But first make me a little cake and bring it to me. Afterwards you can prepare something for yourself and your son. For the Lord, the God of Israel, says: 'The jar of flour shall not go empty, nor the jug of oil run dry, until the day when the Lord sends rain upon the earth.' She left and did as Elijah had said. She had enough to eat for a long time—he and she and her household." (1 Kings 17:10–15)

Elijah tells her to take a leap of faith. She trusts him and obeys, generously feeding the prophet with no guarantee that she wouldn't starve to death afterward. Her gift to the prophet is like the widow's meager donation to the temple.

PREACH TITHING BUT LIVE LIKE A SAINT

You tread a delicate, and even dangerous, line here. You can't be afraid to preach tithing and why it's good for us, but at the same time you can't come across as a greedy wolf who's just looking to add a jacuzzi to the rectory. In very concrete terms, this means YOU must live simply.

I just read a biography of St. Jean-Marie Vianney to my four-year-old. He lived extremely simply, going so far as to wear the same tattered clothes for years. But he did not spare any expense making his church glorious. Take a moment to look up some pictures of the Basilica in Ars. Isn't it glorious? It still draws hundreds of thousands of pilgrims every year from around the world. Do you think the gifts that built that glorious temple to the Most High God were well used? Of course!

Keep in mind that the highest use of any material thing, money included, is the worship of God. Service to the poor comes second, even as the love of neighbor is secondary to love of God. When you are inviting our parishioners to give for the building up of the Church, you are encouraging a virtuous act. An act of faith and an act of worship. And you can't use the excuse that our parish is too poor to pay these maintenance costs. The small gifts of the poor are pleasing to God, and He can make up the difference out of His own infinite bounty.

God will give them what they need, though not everything they want. The primary error of the prosperity preacher is that he focuses on earthly rather than heavenly treasure. Our faith, our life is much bigger than our desire for a big house and a more prestigious job. The riches that God pours out on His beloved are treasures that thieves cannot steal, or rust devour. Faith, hope, love. Heavenly riches that so far exceed the value of anything earthly that it is foolish to try to compare them.

GOD RESPONDS TO OUR PRAYERS AND OUR GIVING

Do you think that the widow in the temple was taken care of after Jesus witnessed her gift? I have no doubt. But more than providing for her material welfare, I bet God answered her prayer in a way that increased her store of heavenly treasure. That built her faith and filled her with love of God that overflowed into praise. Like the fellow who donated to the food bank. He did not doubt that God responded to our prayers and got him a new job. He wrote back just to praise the Lord.

Do you think he got a hundredfold return on his $5? Way more than that. God will always outdo us in generosity.

Blessings,
The Almoner

P.S. To put this perspective into practice, pray about how to preach about heavenly treasure. To stir up people's faith so they can see that the gifts that God wants to give us are more desirable than any earthly thing. Read some of St. Jean-Marie Vianney's sermons. He had a real knack for it.

29.

WHY STEWARDSHIP? A PERSONAL TESTIMONY

Dear Fr. Zagloba,

TO BE HONEST, NO, I don't think most people in the parish have caught hold of vision for the "Stewardship as a Way of Life." Most people I've asked about it say that it sounds like another scheme to raise more money. I have trouble answering this objection because raising more money for the church is one of the good fruits of embracing stewardship as a parish. It doesn't help that churches and dioceses often start pushing stewardship when they have pressing financial needs.

Why am I so passionate about stewardship and giving to the Church? I'm not getting paid. It takes a lot of time and energy that I could be using to learn how to juggle or make toys for my kids. It's stressful, and nobody else gets excited when I'm talking about it. Some people get downright hostile!

STEWARDSHIP—A PATH TO FREEDOM

The way you use your money matters. Obviously. Your spending habits tell you a lot about what you think is important, what you enjoy, what you value. If you spend a great deal of money on rebuilding classic cars, you are making a statement that you believe classic cars are a worthy investment.

What is less obvious is a proverb that has stuck with me for a long time, "What you own, owns you." Those classic cars require expensive maintenance. You might build a garage to protect them from the elements. You pay extra to purchase special insurance. Time you spend working in the garage is time that you don't spend doing other things.

Jesus teaches that we can't serve two masters. We must choose either God or mammon. When our use of money is disordered, when God's priorities don't come first for us in our financial decisions, mammon becomes our master. We become money's slave. How many times have you heard, "I would quit such and such terrible job, but I've got bills to pay"? Or, "I can't go be a missionary, I've got a mortgage." Since money is their master, they are not free to do what God calls them to do.

Stewardship, on the other hand, puts God at the center of financial decisions. Faith becomes the lens through which we view our financial decisions, not fear. Someone who is living stewardship is no longer a slave to Mammon but instead becomes a servant of God. Think for a moment which one YOU want to rule your life. Who do you think is a better master? God Almighty or the (not quite) almighty dollar?

I'm not suggesting that everyone is called to live radical Gospel poverty. I have a wife and children. I must support and provide for them. But fulfilling my financial duty doesn't mean that mammon is my master. Far from it! Instead, I have chosen to let God be my master, especially in the realm of finances.

BREAKING THE CHAINS

I'm talking about freedom in a very concrete sense, not just as an intellectual exercise. I've walked this road. About ten years ago, my finances were a total wreck. I was up to my eyeballs in credit card debt. I defaulted on my student loans. I had collections agencies chasing after me for bills that were past due, but no money to pay them. My credit score tanked. Mammon was my master, and it took me behind the woodshed and gave me a beating.

Shortly after my conversion, a friend of mine introduced me to Compass Catholic Ministries. This ministry teaches people to practice stewardship according to Biblical principles and the teachings of the Church. It points out that the Bible talks a lot about the proper use of money, and that conforming ourselves to a biblical understanding of stewardship can have transformative effects in our lives.

For nine weeks, I got together with a group of friends to watch teachings, discuss homework assignments, and eat a meal. I built some great friendships, but I also came away with a Biblical perspective on how I should manage my money. I realized that I needed to pay off the debts I had foolishly racked up. I needed to change my spending habits so that I didn't buy things that I couldn't afford. I also needed to be generous with the money that God had so generously given me.

The freedom I found though the stewardship way of life is priceless. Ten years later, I have no consumer debt. My student loan balance is a third of what it was five years ago. I buy old cars cash, so I don't have car payments. I give away nearly 20% of my net income. My wife can stay home with our children. And I have an investment portfolio. I live more modestly than I used to, and I'm content.

It's not a magic bullet or a get rich quick scheme, either. Financial stewardship means learning how to manage your finances prudently and make good decisions about what you're doing with your money. It means learning how to budget, and how to assess the difference between your needs and wants in a context of prayer. It requires the often-painful practice of financial discipline and self-denial over the long haul. When you begin to live a stewardship way of life, the way you use and relate to money will change permanently.

During this transition, God has proven to be the most generous master. As I practice financial discipline, He makes room for me to spend money on things that my family and I enjoy. More importantly, I have peace about our finances because I know that God is right in the middle of it. My wife and I don't argue about money because we're on the same page. She has embraced a stewardship way of life as well, and it provides a sense of safety and security for both of us.

A PARISH SET FREE

So why am I willing to invest my time and energy into teaching financial stewardship? I know that it changes lives. Folks in our parish can experience the same kind of liberation that has changed my life. They just need help seeing that God's promises are true. They need someone who has tasted and seen the goodness of the Lord. Someone who will encourage them to call on Jesus and ask Him to bind the strong man Mammon and cast him out of their house.

I think that is something worth doing.

Blessings,
The Almoner

30.

LET'S GO FISHING—ACQUIRING NEW DONORS

Dear Mrs. Sanderson,

I UNDERSTAND HOW HARD it is to set up meetings with people about the food pantry. It's not their top priority. I think you and Mr. Jenson are doing great and should keep it up. I do agree that the $550 a month already committed gives you enough resources to get started. You might have to start out doing one day per month rather than two, but that's still a great start!

In the meantime, I think you should continue doing one-on-one meetings. I think opening the food pantry will probably help you fundraise. You'll get some stories to tell the people when you ask them to donate. It will no longer be something that might happen. It will be happening. That will do a lot to quiet the doubts of skeptical potential donors.

GENTLE, PERSISTENT REMINDERS

I think it's time to include a new strategy to your approach. The person-to-person approach works great, but you need to reach more people in a brief time. The way to do this is to put announcements in the bulletin. They've already heard you talk about it during Mass. I'm sure many people have thought to themselves, "Oh, that sounds like a good idea," but just haven't taken the time to act on it.

The bulletin announcements will bring the food pantry to the top of their minds again. We can talk to Fr. Zagloba and get permission to put in some pictures and a story of our first day of being open. I know that's a month or two away, so in the meantime, we'll just put in a brief invitation to be a part of this excellent work.

You might worry that we're being too persistent and will start to annoy people. That simply isn't the case. People tend to forget ads almost immediately. The marketing geniuses of the world insist that the more people see an ad, the more likely they are to act on it. How often do you see ads for Coca-Cola on TV? On billboards? On the red trucks that drive around town? Online? 10 times a week? 50 times a week? 100 or more times a week? Do these ads make you angry? Or thirsty? When was the last time you grabbed a Coca-Cola from the cooler next to the cash register at the grocery store, just because you saw that red can with those familiar letters?

Doing ads in the bulletin can work in the same way, if we don't get pushy or whiney. We're inviting them to be a part of something awesome, yet it makes sense that people are busy and need help remembering to donate. The more they see our ad, the more likely they will be to take the plunge and donate.

THE KINGDOM OF GOD IS LIKE A NET

Bulletin ads are a simple way of doing what fundraisers call "donor acquisition." Think of donor acquisition as being like the parable of the fishing net:

> Again, the kingdom of heaven is like a net thrown into the sea, which collects fish of every kind. When it is full they haul it ashore and sit down to put what is good into buckets. What is bad they throw away. (Matthew 13:47–48)

Every person that donates after seeing your ad is a fish in the net. Those donors have been "acquired." But your work isn't over after that first donation comes in. Now you start the process of sorting the good from the bad. The good fish are those people who will give again if you thank them properly and ask again. The bad fish are not interested in giving on a more regular basis.

(Now this is not to say that people who only give once are bad people. I'm just using the descriptions from the parable to make the comparison. We're as thankful for the one-time donor as we are to the consistent giver.)

With "big net" donor acquisition, the connection that you're making with people is nowhere near as strong as the connection that you make during a face-to-face meeting. Most people who donate in response to this kind of fundraising are going to be making one-time donations. This is to be expected. But you will need to have a plan to communicate with ALL the donors and sort out those who will continue to give and those who won't.

FINDING AND KEEPING THE GOOD FISH

Email is the pot we'll use to hang onto our good fish. We can get reports from Carmen in the office and use the email addresses they used to give online. I know you said that you hate computers, but maybe we can convince your granddaughter to help. You've said that you're always looking for ways to get her involved at Church. She would need to learn how to use MailChimp, one of the leading e-mail marketing companies. It's a great tool, and for the number of emails we're going to be doing, it's free.

I know. When I start talking about technology your eyes glaze over a bit. But this will be fun. You're going to be writing a monthly letter to your friends about the charitable work that they are doing when they donate. You'll share stories, pictures, ask for prayers, say thank you. I'll work with both of you to come up with a monthly email to everyone who has already donated to the food pantry. Occasionally, but not every time, we'll ask them to give again. We'll even ask them to consider making their gift automatically every month. If they don't give again after a year's worth of emails, we'll let them swim back to sea.

I'll show your granddaughter how to create a separate email list for the people who have already committed to giving every month. Instead of asking every month, we'll just send the thank you note with pictures and a story. We want to make sure that they feel connected to the service that the food pantry is doing. Their gifts make it possible for you to serve. We need to make sure that they know it and know that WE know it. We also want them to be excited and gratified by the success of the food pantry made possible by their gifts.

I think that this approach combined with the person-to-person approach will bring us enough consistent donations for the pantry to get rolling.

Blessings,
The Almoner

P.S. It is probably better to use the phrase "long-term supporters" instead of "good fish" and "one-time donors" instead of "bad fish." Especially if you're talking to anyone else about our plan. The parable just gives such a good illustration of the process of acquiring new donors that I couldn't resist.

31.

STOCKED UP—A PATH TO BIGGER GIFTS

Dear Fr. Zagloba,

I HAVE GREAT NEWS about the matching grant! A few months ago, I mentioned the possibility of getting money from the Catholic Extension Society to help fix the roof. They approved us for $10,000! This is great!

Since it's a matching grant, we're going to have to raise money before we get the grant. The terms of the match are that they'll match one dollar for every two dollars we raise. To get the full $10,000, we'll have to raise $20,000. We have six months to raise the funding, so we'll want to start right away.

We should do a 'fundraising goal' display in the narthex that charts our progress, as well as information in the bulletin, a weekly social media update with how much closer we are to the goal, and weekly announcements during Mass. We need to tell people about the need and the matching funds that are available.

LOCK, STOCK, AND BARREL

I think that St. Catherine's also needs a stockbroker. Hear me out. I don't think that we should start day-trading to try to hit our goal. That would be about as prudent as using our donations to purchase lottery tickets. Crazy! Instead, the stock account will open a whole new way to take donations.

I'm not sure how many of our parishioners own stock, but I'd venture a guess that it's more than you expect. Especially among our retirees. I know from my research that one of the big issues for retirees is that they hold a significant percentage of their assets in stocks. They have a problem when it comes to unrealized capital gains.

Say they bought 50 shares of stock in 1980 at $10 per share that now sells for $150 per share. The initial $500 investment is now worth $7,500. Selling those stocks creates a $7,000 tax liability (the difference between the stock's current value and its purchase price). Depending on their tax rate, they'll have to pay somewhere between $700 and $1,400 in taxes. The tax liability reduces the amount they can donate, as well as the amount that they will be able to deduct. It might even push them into a higher tax bracket and force them to pay higher taxes on ALL their income. It's a lose-lose-lose situation.

Not to worry: there's a better way. If we set up a stock account, then they can make a gift of the shares directly to the account. Since they aren't selling the stock, no taxable event takes place. Our account manager will then liquidate the stock, and we can transfer the funds to our bank account. The donor will get the full tax benefit of their donation, without any of the tax liability. It's a win-win-win situation!

We'll need to let people know about this new option, so once it's available, you'll need to tell them about it during announcements. We can also put the information in the bulletin, and if you'd like we can put together a brochure about stock gifts for the lobby display shelf. The important thing is to get the word out that we're able to do it.

You can probably get a self-managed stock account which is technically cheaper, but I think we need a human broker. Sometimes these gift transactions can be confusing, and it is worth the expense to have a professional do it for us.

Blessings,
The Almoner

P.S. Check with the Diocese. Come to think of it, they might have a way to accept and liquidate stock gifts that won't require us setting up or managing anything. We might be able to just publicize it and take the proceeds of the gifts when they arrive.

32.

TAKE ARMS AGAINST A SEA OF MAMMON

Dear Fr. Zagloba,

I CAN ALMOST SEE you rolling your eyes at me. "Not another way to give ... no more bulletin announcements!" I understand fundraising is not your favorite thing and you are rightly concerned that you don't want people to think that money is your only concern. There's a real danger of people thinking that you're only looking for another way to squeeze another dime out of their pocket.

But let's look at this with a more spiritual perspective. Part of the reason that the money conversation is so hard in parish life is that it's right on the front lines in the battle between God and Mammon. Jesus said "No one can serve two masters. He will either hate one and love the other, or be devoted to one and despise the other. You cannot serve God and mammon" (Matthew 6:24). Mammon, of course, means money or material possessions.

Of course, any preaching that touches on giving to the Church has the potential to stir up a hornet's nest. The spirit of Mammon may dominate our age more than any period in human history. Our culture glories in and celebrates the lives of billionaires, while the lives of the Saints collect dust on the shelf. Rich is the new holy. And we wonder why our culture despises their Divine Savior. Jesus told us that this is the way it works.

When you engage in fundraising at our parish, you are taking the forces of Mammon captive and bringing them to serve the kingdom of the Redeemer. Mammon is not going to give up without a fight.

THE TRUTH WILL SET YOU FREE

Let's be honest. Very few of our parishioners are paying a full tithe of 10%. Maybe a dozen. The rest are falling short in their giving. Part of the reason that people get upset when you start talking about money is that they feel convicted. On some level, they know they should be giving more but choose not to for whatever reason.

It doesn't help that there's a lot of confusion about tithing in the Church. Most people don't know what the Church teaches, or, if they do, they misunderstand or misinterpret it. Part of the current confusion comes from the fact that the Code of Canon Law from 1983 is not explicit in describing the duty to tithe. It states:

> Can. 222 §1. The Christian faithful are obliged to assist with the needs of the Church so that the Church has what is necessary for divine worship, for the works of the apostolate and of charity, and for the decent support of ministers.
>
> §2. They are also obliged to promote social justice and, mindful of the precept of the Lord, to assist the poor from their own resources.

You see in these two statements my mantra, "Give to the Church and to the poor." But it doesn't say "tithe" and it doesn't say "10% of your income," so people can quibble about the actual duty to give that much. I've heard our bishop suggest that we give 5% to the Church and 5% to other ministries of mercy, but I can't find that written down anywhere. In "Stewardship: A Disciple's Response," the US Bishops said:

> One of the most frequently asked questions in any stewardship educational program is "How much do I have to give?" The answer (from a stewardship perspective) is nothing. We don't have to give anything.

If you tell people that nothing is expected of them, expect them to do nothing. Why do you think that giving in the Catholic Church is so abysmal? We don't ask our parishioners to tithe, and as a result, they don't tithe.

Notre Dame published a study on giving in church called "Unleashing Catholic Generosity" a few years ago. How do you think Catholics fared compared with other religious denominations? Terribly! 15% of Catholics reported that they tithed, compared with 75% of Mormons, 44% of Evangelical Protestants, 35% of African American Protestants, 20% of Mainline Protestants, and 18% of Jews. Why are these other groups successfully promoting tithing, but the Church is not? Do they have more money? No! They're just talking about tithing. They're asking their people to tithe. And guess what? Their people tithe!

GO BACK TO THE BEGINNING!

People need to hear from the pulpit that tithing is part of being a disciple. It started in the Old Testament and continues into the present day. Tithing appears for the first time in the book of Genesis. Abraham tithed when he gave Melchizedek one-tenth of the booty he captured when he rescued his nephew Lot from the five kings.

> Melchizedek, king of Salem, brought out bread and wine. He was a priest of God Most High. He blessed Abram with these words: "Blessed be Abram by God Most High, the creator of heaven and earth; And blessed be God Most High, who delivered your foes into your hand." Then Abram gave him a tenth of everything. (Genesis 14:18–20).

The reference to Melchizedek is very significant. His offering of bread and wine prefigures the Eucharist of the New Covenant. The Letter to the Hebrews points out that Christ has become the High Priest according to the order of Melchizedek (Hebrews 6:20). Thus, Abram's tithing to Melchizedek points towards a similar duty to give a tenth part of our own produce to our High Priest through the Church that He founded. Given how supremely superior our High Priest's offering of His own Body and Blood is to the bread and wine offered by His predecessor, how great is our own duty to give our High Priest His due?

In Leviticus, Moses teaches the specifics of tithing and includes God's justification for the tithe. Tithes are sacred.

> All tithes of the land, whether in grain from the fields or in fruit from the trees, BELONG TO THE LORD (my emphasis); they are sacred to the LORD. If someone wishes to redeem any of the tithes, the person shall pay one-fifth more than their value. The tithes of the herd and the flock, every tenth animal that passes under the herdsman's rod, shall be sacred to the LORD. It shall not matter whether good ones or bad ones are thus chosen, and no exchange may be made. If any exchange is made, both the original animal and its substitute become sacred and cannot be redeemed. (Leviticus 27:30–34)

Clarity is so important. God claims the tenth part as His own.

My least favorite Church fundraising proverb, "It all belongs to God anyway," is incorrect. God isn't that greedy. He gives us everything, of course, but according to what He instructed us through Moses, He limits His ownership to the tithe. He confirms His ownership through the prophet Malachi:

> But you say, "Why should we return? Can anyone rob God?" But you are robbing me! And you say, "How have we robbed you?" Of tithes and contributions! You are indeed accursed, for you, the whole nation, rob me. Bring the whole tithe into the storehouse, that there may be food in my house. Put me to the test, says the Lord of hosts, and see if I do not open the floodgates of heaven for you, and pour down upon you blessing without measure! I will rebuke the locust for you so that it will not destroy your crops, and the vine in the field will not be barren, says the Lord of hosts. All the nations will call you blessed, for you will be a delightful land, says the Lord of hosts. (Malachi 3:8–12)

God uses the prophet to connect the dots for them by pointing out that those who tithe are blessed and those who steal the tithe for themselves are accursed. He tells them to try tithing, that He will pour out enormous blessings on them if only they will bring their offerings into the storehouse.

Jesus even went far beyond tithing. The story of the rich young man is a great example:

> Jesus said to him, "If you wish to be perfect, go, sell what you have and give to the poor, and you will have treasure in heaven. Then come, follow me." When the young man heard this statement, he went away sad, for he had many possessions. (Matthew 19:21–22)

Jesus didn't just want the 10%, He wanted everything. The young man's big problem is that he didn't have enough faith to see that treasure in Heaven is worth more than everything that he could give.

Again, Jesus goes beyond the tithe when he says, "Whoever has two tunics should share with the person who has none. And whoever has food should do likewise" (Luke 3:11). If you have two garments and give one away, that's giving half. And who, when sharing a meal, gives away a measly 10%?

And if you think Jesus condemns tithing when He rebukes the Pharisees, you're not reading it closely enough.

> Woe to you Pharisees! You pay tithes of mint and of rue and of every garden herb, but you pay no attention to judgment and to love for God. These you should have done, without overlooking the others. (Luke 11:42)

Jesus tells them that tithing, justice, mercy, and faithfulness are all tied together. You can't do just one of the four and think that you're off the hook. But that doesn't mean that you can overlook tithing. He doesn't free them from their responsibility to give their tithes to the Church.

The Church has also perennially taught tithing. Did you know that the Council of Trent excommunicated Catholics who don't tithe?

> Tithes to be paid in full: those withholding, or hindering, the payment thereof are to be excommunicated: the Rectors of Poor Churches are to be piously relieved. (Decree of Reformation, Chapter XII)

That Council took tithing very seriously, and it should not be misinterpreted as a financial shakedown of the faithful. The Church has a divine mandate to instruct the faithful on how we are to live the Gospel. If they did not strongly enforce the divine commandment, they would be guilty of trying to please men rather than God. Excommunication serves as a remedy with the goal of bringing about repentance and the restoration of full communion. In our own day, both the new Catechism (paragraph 2043) and Code of Canon Law (Canon 222) speak of the obligation of the faithful to support the Church.

The teaching of Scripture and Tradition clearly and compellingly state that tithing is part of being a disciple. And it's not just an obligation, but a source of tremendous blessing for the faithful. We don't just HAVE to give a tithe offering to God, we GET to do so.

PREACHING TITHING WORKS!

One of the things I've heard over and again is that discussions of tithing will scare parishioners off. This simply is not true. How do I know? Because it works in so many Protestant Churches.

Do you ever get frustrated by the fact that the Baptist Church down the road has three times as many staff members as we do, even though they are the same size? This is because they preach tithing. The preachers expect people to give, they teach people to give, and—shock of all shocks—people give. They give willingly. They give generously. And as a result, that Baptist Church can hire a full-time youth minister to run the programs that end up serving OUR children.

Catholics these days are so scared of the money conversation that they give up before even trying. Do remember from your native Poland how many little tiny villages had big beautiful churches in their hearts? These were not built by rich people. They were built by people who loved the Church and believed that their gifts to the Church had a divine purpose. They were moved by God's perfect Sacrifice to give of themselves, even as the offering of Melchizedek inspired the first recorded tithe.

TITHING IS A MARTIAL ART

Understand that when you preach giving according to God's commandments, the kingdom of Mammon screams in protest. The world, the flesh, and the devil will oppose you with great ferocity. You are engaging in spiritual combat, and your weapon against confusion and inaction is the truth. You need to pray in advance for the grace to conquer. Your armor in this battle is charity, meekness and humility. Remember that instructing the ignorant is a work of mercy. They might not like it, they might protest, but ultimately you have their best interest at heart. You are on a rescue mission, and Mammon is the big bad guy that we must conquer if we want to enjoy the glorious freedom of the children of God.

Blessings,
The Almoner

P.S. Now let's face the fact that we are not going to win the fight against Mammon all at once. Most people in the parish don't have their lives arranged in such a way that they can start giving 10% of their income to the Church. Encourage them to start somewhere, maybe 1%, and grow as they are able. You have to win a battle before you can win the war. God is on their side and will grow their generosity as time goes on.

33.

CONVERSIONS FOR THE WEB AND THE SOUL

Dear Fr. Zagloba,

I'VE BEEN THINKING about the parish's website. Online donations have been slowly but steadily increasing, which is great. Unfortunately, we still don't use the web to do much of anything. Our site is just an online bulletin board with some useful information posted. The beauty of the web is that it can be interactive. What I want to do is re-imagine what the website can do. We have a big opportunity here, but we need to have a vision for it.

The basic idea is to use the website to drive engagement at the parish. "Engagement" is a marketing word that means the two-way communication and interaction between an individual and an organization. Right now, the Mass each week is the primary way people have contact with the Church. Some might "engage" by joining the Knights of Columbus or the Council of Catholic Women. Try to think of engagement as the level of connection people have with the parish and the degree to which their faith affects their lives.

STARTING A CONVERSATION THAT LEADS TO CONVERSION

Think of engagement like a conversation between the Church] and each parishioner. Each conversation is unique because each person in our parish is in a different place in their journey of faith. Our job with the website is to create something that comes alongside them and walks with them.

In the world of web design, the word 'conversion' means that a person who comes to your website does something that you want them to do. For a news site, conversion might be signing up for a weekly newsletter. For an online business, conversion means that the visitor makes a purchase. For our website, conversion means—you guessed it—conversion. We want people who come to our website to experience conversion and either begin the life of faith or start to live their faith more fully.

How do we use web conversions to bring about spiritual conversions? We have a couple of different groups of people or audiences that we should keep in mind. The first and biggest are members of St. Catherine's. A second audience is people who are new in town that are looking for a Catholic church in their area. A third audience is people who have been invited to check out St. Catherine's but who are not currently Catholic. A fourth audience is Catholics who have left the faith and are interested in returning. A fifth audience is members of the parish who have immediate pastoral needs.

Looking at these different audiences, I can see a few different places on the 'journey of faith' where we can meet them with the website and engage their interest.

Stage 1—Welcome—The first stage is welcoming them to the parish and getting them either registered if they're already Catholic or connecting them with faith formation if they are interested in becoming Catholic. The web conversion here is to get their e-mail address and contact information.

Stage 2—Initiation—The second stage is bringing people to an understanding of the faith that is sufficient for them to enter the sacramental life of the Church. The web conversion at this stage might be to take a survey about where they are in their sacramental life. Another web conversion might be to sign up for sacramental prep classes.

Stage 3—Discipleship—The third stage is enabling church members to grow in their life of faith through prayer, study, and works of mercy. This stage should include learning resources as well as invitations to participate in (or even create) ministries that reach outside the walls of the Church carrying the light of the Gospel. A web conversion might be getting them to sign up for a Church ministry or linking them to a website with faith formation resources.

Stage 4—Pastoral Care—The fourth stage is for folks who need help or assistance in either their lives of faith or are going through a time of crisis. It might be people who are in the hospital who need the sacraments brought to them, or it might be people looking for resources that can help them save their marriage. The web conversion here is for them to give us their information and tell us how we can serve their needs.

TOOLS AND TEMPLATES

Our website can be a place where people come to learn about their faith, connect with others, and get involved in the mission of the Church. We should probably scrap what we have entirely and start over. I think our current website was written in HTML about 15 years ago, which is the computer equivalent of running a NASCAR race on a donkey.

There's a tool out there called 'WordPress' that will allow us to build the website for free, or mostly free. I know that we don't have the money to hire a web developer, but perhaps if you ask during Mass, someone in the parish who knows how to build WordPress websites will raise their hand.

I've been learning to use WordPress, and it is great fun. One of the best parts is that you can make it look the way you want. Hundreds of free themes are available that determine what the main page and all of the secondary pages look like, where pictures can go, and what fonts you use. It gives you a basic layout structure that you can then fill with content. If you want to add additional cool functionality, WordPress also has thousands of mini-programs called plugins that you can then use to make it do cool things like collect email addresses or manage event invitations.

For starters, Google "Best WordPress Church Themes." It will bring up an enormous number of different Church themes for you to sort through. Most of them allow you to try it out so you can see if you like the functionality. Find two or three designs that you like, and we can sit down and talk about them. Once you find two or three that you like, we can start talking about our next steps forward.

Blessings,
The Almoner

P.S. Realize that this is a long-term project. Even with a professional web developer, building a new website can take six months to a year. We'll be moving slowly because it's an all-volunteer effort, but we'll get there.

34.

CRYING OUT FOR MERCY

Dear Fr. Zagloba,

AT MASS SUNDAY, something struck me with a force of a blow. Kyrie Eleison. Lord, have mercy. I have never thought about this before because I'm not a Greek scholar, but eleison comes from the same Greek word as eleemosyne, the word that means alms. The word eleison is used in the Gospel passage when blind Bartimaeus is calling to the Lord for mercy.

The Holy Mass puts the words of a beggar in our mouths at the very beginning of every celebration. "Lord, have mercy." We are blind, wretched, in need of alms, of mercy. And so, I cry out, "Kyrie eleison. Christe eleison. Kyrie eleison."

WE ARE ALL BEGGARS BEFORE CHRIST

How humbling it is to recognize our position before God! Beggars! We're all beggars crying out, "Lord, have mercy!" when we hear that He is near. And His response—He draws close to us. In Scripture and sacramental sign, He becomes present to us, finding fulfillment in a perfect and complete gift of Himself—communion.

We don't deserve it. We haven't earned it. We can't repay Him. He opens our eyes to His merciful love and grants us our heart's desire. Eternal life and perpetual beatitude.

Recognizing our need for mercy, for the Merciful One, is what it means to be poor in spirit. To beg without shame. To cry out at the top of our lungs, LORD HAVE MERCY, even when the surrounding crowds and the disciples tell us to be silent. To recognize that our need for mercy is greater than our need for approval, or recognition, or honor. To become aware of our poverty and our need for our Savior.

ALMS ARE INCARNATE MERCY

When we're fundraising and asking people to support the ministries of the Church, we are entering this mystery. We become the voice of the voiceless. Or to use an even more powerful image, we're like the four fellows who lowered their paralyzed friend into the home where Jesus could demonstrate His healing power.

I think many people know their need for mercy, but don't know the Lord of Mercy. As fundraisers, we are asking for alms, for mercy, on their behalf. Those alms enable mercy that you can touch, taste, and see. Churches feed the spiritual needs of the poor in spirit. Hospitals minister to the physically sick. Food pantries fill empty tummies.

Mercy is not abstract, i.e., a simple absence of punishment deserved. Mercy is incarnational. It enters the lives of the poor and meets their immediate needs. The story of the good Samaritan illustrates the concreteness of mercy in such a vivid way. Mercy means stopping what we're doing, getting off our donkeys, and doing something to help the bloody and beaten man lying beside the road.

SOLIDARITY WITH THE POOR

Kyrie eleison. I am a beggar. I stand with other beggars, not above them. I belong with them. We have pierced to the heart of solidarity with the poor. Once I recognize that all are beggars before God, myself included, I can begin to treat everyone I meet like a long-lost brother or sister. This is the foundation of charity.

Blessings,
The Almoner

35.

BE A GRATEFUL LEPER

Dear Mrs. Sanderson,

CONGRATULATIONS ON THE food pantry's first day of ministry! What a blessing to finally open the doors after all this time planning and preparing. I think that providing food to 35 families on your first day is a wonderful accomplishment. No, I don't think it's a problem that we ran out of food. You're not stockpiling food for an emergency. You're trying to give it away to people who are already in an emergency. You didn't have to send anyone home empty-handed, which is what matters.

I could tell by the expression on your face as we closed up that you were more than satisfied with the result. You're hooked. You expected to feed all those people, but you had no idea how much this ministry would feed you! I'm so delighted that I've been able to help you discover and establish the ministry that God intended. I can't wait to see what you'll be doing in the years to come.

SHARE THE JOY

We need to come up with a way to share the joy of this experience with the rest of the parish, especially with those whose time and donations made it possible. I want your glow to rub off on them, and the stories of the good their gifts enabled are a wonderful way to help them share the excitement.

The first best way to thank people is to do it directly. You would need to make 42 phone calls to say thank you personally to all our donors. Since this is the very first day that the ministry served people, I think it's appropriate. The excitement and joy in your voice will convey something that is very hard to write down or convey in any other way.

I also think that we should ask Fr. Zagloba for permission to speak after Mass and share a little bit about our experience of serving the community. Not a huge presentation, just 3–4 minutes to share from the heart how wonderful it was to feed the hungry and thank the whole parish for supporting the ministry. This public "thank you," with all the joy and enthusiasm that fills you right now, will have a powerful effect on encouraging others to get involved as donors and volunteers.

COMMITMENT TO GRATITUDE

In the long-term, expressing your gratitude to the ministry's supporters should be an important, regular activity. While I don't think a phone call is necessary every month, I do think that a thank you letter or email for every monthly gift is more than appropriate. Your thank you notes are a way to keep people connected to what you're doing. You can share a little bit about the number of people whom you served, but the story of a person that you met while ministering would be even more powerful. Numbers are fine. I use them a lot in grant writing, but they just don't have the impact that a personal story or testimony will have.

You should plan on a personal connection at least once a year, either face-to-face or over the phone. During the holiday season is probably best, although you'll want to do it starting in early November to avoid the busyness of the Advent Season. You can reconnect with your supporters and it will give you an opportunity to share about all the good that you've been able to do throughout the year with their help.

During the rest of the year, you can do emails with a thank you, story, and picture. Something personal that people will enjoy reading. It's great to share the exciting things that happen, but don't be afraid to share some of the hard things that happen. Ministry to the poor is not always easy and sharing stories that move you can also help our donors feel connected to what we're doing.

Expressing your gratitude helps people to know and feel that they are more than a source of revenue for the pantry. They are supporters. Members of a team that is feeding the hungry. A side effect of a consistent effort to thank your donors is that you'll see more repeat donations. But this is not so much about increasing donations as telling our supporters about the good that they're doing with their gifts.

ONE IN TEN

The story of Jesus with the ten lepers comes to mind.

> As he continued his journey to Jerusalem, he traveled through Samaria and Galilee. As he was entering a village, ten lepers met him. They stood at a distance from him and raised their voice, saying, "Jesus, Master! Have pity on us!" And when he saw them, he said, "Go show yourselves to the priests." As they were going they were cleansed. And one of them, realizing he had been healed, returned, glorifying God in a loud voice; and he fell at the feet of Jesus and thanked him. He was a Samaritan. Jesus said in reply, "Ten were cleansed, were they not? Where are the other nine? Has none but this foreigner returned to give thanks to God?" Then he said to him, "Stand up and go; your faith has saved you." (Luke 17:11–19)

All the lepers got healed. Only one came back and said thank you. Jesus praised the one grateful leper, but then wondered, where are all the rest? I think our donors can sometimes feel like the Lord did. Most give to several different organizations, but how many of these organizations take the time to stop and say thank you?

By going back to your donors with thanks and praise reports, you recognize that this wouldn't have happened without them. They should be proud and excited about what happened because they responded generously. This story points out that this is important!

There's one more thank you that you must not neglect. The Lord called you into this ministry. He's opening the doors to make it possible. First and foremost, we should give thanks to God for bringing this ministry to life. It's His mission and His grace that makes it possible, and it's His love that will make it fruitful and keep it going when it gets tough. Give thanks to the Lord, for He is good! His mercies endure forever.

Congratulations again on Day 1 of the St. Catherine's Food Pantry. It's truly something to celebrate!

Blessings,
The Almoner

36.

STEWARDSHIP IS ONLY 10% ABOUT CHURCH

Dear Fr. Zagloba,

I ATE LUNCH with Mrs. Sanderson yesterday, and we got to talking about doing a stewardship renewal campaign at St. Catherine's. She told me, "Whenever anyone starts talking about stewardship, I hide my wallet." I had to laugh. It's a stereotype, but let's face it, most parishes start breaking out Stewardship when their revenue figures start to dip.

I think a lot of parishes, and perhaps even more stewardship consultants, approach stewardship with the primary goal of increasing a church's bottom line. They might be doing so with the best of intentions and trying to help people to live their faith more completely. But fundraising consultants typically have targets to hit and are less invested in the actual life of the parish, so there is the real danger that they will steer any campaign towards a purely fundraising focus.

TITHING IS 10%, WHAT ABOUT THE OTHER 90%?

What's the right focus? I've told you before that learning about stewardship and beginning to practice stewardship was a real turning point in my life. And honestly, beginning to give more of my money to the Church was a small part of the total transformation. About 10%. The real revolution that stewardship started in my life had to do with the other 90%.

Most of our parishioners spend significantly less than 10% of their money and their time at St. Catherine's. They spend most of their lives and most of their money outside of the walls of this Church. If you convinced every person to give a full tithe and come to daily Mass, it still would be a small fraction of their resources and their time. You don't want Jesus to just be the Lord of the Sabbath, you want Him to be Lord of the whole week. As the old preacher's proverb goes, "If He's not Lord of all, He's not Lord AT all!"

An authentic call to stewardship should meet people where they are—in the 90%—where they're struggling to make their rent or mortgage payment, pay tuition, or cover medical bills. Or they want to build a retirement fund or save to send kids to college. Stewardship helps us to bring the financial aspect of our lives under the Lordship of Jesus Christ. Focus on the fact that stewardship gives them more peace in their finances.

DON'T SETTLE FOR THE PHARISEE'S PORTION

Mrs. Sanderson pointed out that Jesus chastised the Pharisees for focusing on the 10% but then neglecting the 90%. They were tithing their spice garden's mint, dill, and cumin, but they were neglecting the more important things, justice, mercy, and faithfulness. Jesus doesn't diminish the importance of tithing in this passage because He says that they should continue to do so. But He expands their responsibility to include the rest of the 90%.

This passage points out that our stewardship efforts should focus on what Jesus gives priority—justice, mercy, and faithfulness—with the understanding the tithing should naturally accompany these three virtues.

First—Justice. Give to another what is due to them. The Bible contains many wise sayings that help us to understand justice as it pertains to financial stewardship.

> False scales are an abomination to the LORD, but an honest weight, his delight. (Proverbs 11:1)

> Do not keep with you overnight the wages of those who have worked for you, but pay them at once. If you serve God thus, you will receive your reward. (Sirach 4:14)

Church teaching expands on these types of proverbs to teach us how to be just financial stewards and just businessmen. In the Summa, St. Thomas Aquinas states, "justice is a habit whereby a man renders to each one his due by a constant and perpetual will" (Sum II-II, Q 58, Ar. 1). This means an understanding of the rights given by God to men and acting accordingly. Specifically, justice is the virtue contrary to the vice forbidden by the commandment, "You shall not steal" (Exodus 20:15).

Second—Mercy. Give generously to the poor and afflicted. Care for the widow, the orphan, and the alien (immigrant) in your midst.

> Give alms from your possessions. Do not turn your face away from any of the poor, so that God's face will not be turned away from you. Give in proportion to what you own. If you have great wealth, give alms out of your abundance; if you have but little, do not be afraid to give alms even of that little. You will be storing up a goodly treasure for yourself against the day of adversity. (Tobit 4:7–9)

Not because they deserve it, but because we have been the recipients of so much of God's generosity that it must overflow to others. I am practicing mercy when I give to someone who can never repay me, trusting that God is pleased when I do so.

Third—Faithfulness. The faithful steward takes good care of anything that has been entrusted to him, knowing that he will have to return it to his Master when the time of his stewardship comes to an end. I care for things differently when I know they belong to someone else and I am going to be held accountable.

> But when he returned after obtaining the kingship, he had the servants called, to whom he had given the money, to learn what they had gained by trading. The first came forward and said, "Sir, your gold coin has earned ten additional ones." He replied, "Well done, good servant! You have been faithful in this very small matter; take charge of ten cities." Then the second came and reported, "Your gold coin, sir, has earned five more." And to this servant too he said, "You, take charge of five cities." Then the other servant came and said, "Sir, here is your gold coin; I kept it stored away in a handkerchief, for I was afraid of you, because you are a demanding

person; you take up what you did not lay down and you harvest what you did not plant." He said to him, "With your own words I shall condemn you, you wicked servant. You knew I was a demanding person, taking up what I did not lay down and harvesting what I did not plant; why did you not put my money in a bank? Then on my return I would have collected it with interest." And to those standing by he said, "Take the gold coin from him and give it to the servant who has ten." But they said to him, "Sir, he has ten gold coins." I tell you, to everyone who has, more will be given, but from the one who has not, even what he has will be taken away. (Luke 19:15–26)

At the time of accounting, there will be a reward for the faithful and punishment for the unfaithful. The faithful steward's reward is not the goods in themselves, but rather something far greater. In Luke's parable the servant who returned ten coins is given authority over ten cities by his master as a reward for his faithfulness. The unfaithful steward gets stripped of all that he has and watches as it is given over to the faithful one.

Faithfulness also includes trusting what God says about money and possessions.

Blessed are you who are poor, for the kingdom of God is yours. (Luke 6:20)

Learn from the way the wild flowers grow. They do not work or spin. But I tell you that not even Solomon in all his splendor was clothed like one of them. (Matthew 6:28–29)

Ask, and you shall receive. (Luke 11:9)

But seek first the kingdom of God, and His righteousness and all these things will be given you besides. (Matthew 6:33)

Faithfulness from this perspective means viewing our finances with the eyes of faith in an all-powerful God who promised to take care of us as a good Father will in fact do so.

Can you see how a focus on these three pillars of stewardship would transform a person's life? How would they transform our parish, and maybe even our city?

A PROBLEM OF IMPLEMENTATION

How can we help people integrate justice, mercy, and faithfulness into their everyday lives? This question should be the focus of our stewardship efforts. In the midst of this, it will be ok to talk about tithing—about 10% of the time.

Compass Catholic Ministries is a great organization for teaching the principles of everyday stewardship. They provide materials to host small-group bible studies that meet for nine weeks to learn and begin to implement stewardship practices in everyday life. Search online for Compass Catholic Ministries and take a look at the materials they've created. Their program changed the way I live my life.

Blessings,
The Almoner

37.

WHO ARE YOUR DISCIPLES?

Dear Fr. Zagloba,

I'M GLAD THAT you took the time to look at Compass Catholic's materials. I love their approach to teaching the practical aspects of stewardship. One reason their small group approach is so powerful is because it uses the same model that Jesus used with His disciples.

I don't know if you've ever thought about it, but Jesus is the pioneer of the small group model. He started out with throngs of people who followed him. Too many people. He prayerfully winnowed it down to just twelve who would have the opportunity to be in His "small group." The truth is you can't build close relationships and have accountability with large groups of people. Even God Himself can't do it (or at least chose not to). Forming disciples requires forming close relationships, which can't be done on a massive scale.

MAKE DISCIPLES (IN SMALL BATCHES)

If you really want stewardship to take off, I think you should lead the first small group. Follow the model that Jesus gave you and ask God in prayer who should be the first dozen couples to go through the Compass Catholic program with you. God will point a couple out to you and give you the sense that you should ask them to join. Or their names and faces might come to mind during your time in adoration. God wants you to succeed and will inspire you to pick people that He has prepared for the task. You should tell the people you ask that you want to train them to be stewardship leaders who can train at least one more group of parishioners with the program. Once you're doing teaching them to be disciples, you're going to send them forth to make MORE disciples.

Trailblazing Compass Catholic Stewardship personally will give you the best possible perspective on the program. Let's face it, if you haven't gone through the program, how can you possibly expect anyone else to participate? Leading the first group will give you a shared vocabulary with future leaders and participants. You'll know the main concepts and will be working from the same playbook. It will also give you the opportunity to build close relationships with a small group of parishioners, which is invaluable in and of itself. You might decide to lead future groups simply because it gives you a chance to connect more closely with an ever-growing number of parishioners.

This might be a little outside of your comfort zone, but don't worry. I think that this will be an immensely satisfying way to practice your ministry. It follows in the footsteps of the Master. How could you go wrong?

A QUESTION OF OWNERSHIP

One word of caution. As you're looking through the Compass Catholic materials, I want you to pay special attention to the section that says, "God owns everything." I've struggled with this phrase as a fundraiser, particularly because I've heard fundraisers in a Church setting use it to beat people over the head during the parish appeals.

People react strongly to the suggestion that they don't own the stuff that they have invested so much time and energy accumulating. If they are not already living stewardship, this idea will sound foreign if not outright hostile to their well-being. With one sentence, you have just stripped them of everything they possess. A little delicacy is appropriate.

The social teaching of the church supports the idea of private property but frames it in the context of our responsibility to care for one another. Pope Leo XII makes this fine distinction in his brilliant encyclical *Rerum Novarum:*

> Private ownership, as we have seen, is the natural right of man, and to exercise that right, especially as members of society, is not only lawful, but absolutely necessary.

> "It is lawful," says St. Thomas Aquinas, "for a man to hold private property; and it is also necessary for the carrying on of human existence." But if the question be asked: How must one's possessions be used?—the Church replies without hesitation in the words of the same holy Doctor: "Man should not consider his material possessions as his own, but as common to all, so as to share them without hesitation when others are in need. Whence the apostle saith, 'Command the rich of this world ... to offer with no stint, to apportion largely.'"

Here you see the concepts of private property and stewardship working in perfect harmony. We hold private property but shouldn't cling to it. God created all things, and everything that we have is a gift from Him. His gifts are not simply to enrich us or make our lives easy. The Pope, the Saint, and the Apostle agree that those who are rich should embrace generosity without limits.

IN THE WORLD BUT NOT OF THE WORLD

As stewards, we must cultivate the proper attitude towards our material goods. According to the ways of the world, we do own our material possessions and have a responsibility to take care of them. Being a Catholic does not absolve you of having to pay your mortgage on time or insure your car. But as citizens of heaven, we shouldn't cling to money or possessions. We need the heart of a steward that recognizes God as the source and Lord of all created things. Since God is so immeasurably generous, we should be prepared to give more than we think is prudent or even possible.

There's a war in our hearts between the love of money and the love of God. The story of the rich young man points it out so clearly:

> An official asked him this question, "Good teacher, what must I do to inherit eternal life?" Jesus answered him, "Why do you call me good? No one is good but God alone. You know the commandments, 'You shall not commit adultery; you shall not kill; you shall not steal; you shall not bear false witness; honor your father and your mother.'" And he replied, "All of these I have observed from my youth." When Jesus heard this he said to him, "There is still one thing left for you: sell all that you have and distribute it to the poor, and you will have a treasure in heaven.

Then come, follow me." But when he heard this he became quite sad, for he was very rich. (Luke 18:18–23)

Jesus gave him the choice between his riches and eternal life, and eternal life LOST! You should never discount the power that the love of money has over humankind. The love of money is the root of all evil, meaning that it enables every conceivable type of sin and disorder to flourish. Becoming a good steward means putting the love of money to death so that our hearts are completely open for the love of God.

Stewardship is the path that leads us to true freedom from the consumerism and materialism that is so deeply rooted in our culture. But don't expect people to give up their 'isms' without a struggle. That's where your personal participation can make such a huge difference. You'll be walking with them, taking the exact same steps that they are, showing them that it IS possible to conquer mammon in their lives.

Being a good shepherd means seeing the wolves that are attacking your flock and sending them running with a few well-placed projectiles. Is there any bigger wolf in our culture than mammon?

HANDCRAFTED DISCIPLES

Leading the first small group (and subsequent sessions if you can) will help you clear your mind of all the administrative details of that often capture your attention. You'll be able to focus on the mission that God Himself gave you. To make disciples. Don't worry. I think you'll love it.

Blessings,
The Almoner

P.S. I'm not denying that it will at times be a cross. People are messy. Being in their lives can be messy. Loving messy people is a cross. But it's the cross that makes us holy, that makes us like Jesus.

38.

INVEST IN ALABASTER JARS

Dear Fr. Zagloba,

HAPPY THANKSGIVING! I hope you have a nice trip to visit your family. We're going to have a house full. Maybe 30 people. 15 or so children. Delightful mayhem.

I've been giving some thought to the question that you raised during the Pastoral Council Meeting. Where should we be investing our money as a parish? What ministries should we be focusing on, and which ones would benefit from some additional funding?

THE PURPOSE OF A CHURCH

What is the central purpose of our church? Not the Church in general—that's a much bigger question. I'm talking about our church, the building that we call St. Catherine's. Why does it exist and how does that factor into the financial decisions that you as the pastor have to make?

You should be able to answer this question easily. The purpose of the building is to serve as a house of worship. It's a spiritual hub where we celebrate the most important events of our lives. The Holy Mass. Baptisms. Confirmations. Weddings. Funerals. The return of prodigal sons. The Mass in and of itself is the most important thing that happens anywhere on earth at any time. Heaven is wedded to earth. To be used in the worship of God is the highest purpose for any material thing, and to be consecrated for use in the Holy Mass changes things. That's the reason we can never use the implements used for the celebration of the Mass for anything else. You know all of this.

It makes sense to invest in the church and make sure that it is a beautiful place for these events. Not because human beings deserve a fitting place to celebrate, but because God is worthy of the very best that we have to offer. The parishioners get to enjoy the benefits of our desire to honor God.

AN EXAMPLE OF LAVISH LOVE

This past summer, I visited the Shrine of the Most Blessed Sacrament in Alabama. Mother Angelica built it to honor Jesus in the Most Blessed Sacrament. She spared no expense. They covered the entire altar piece in gold. I believe the monstrance is encrusted with gems. It may be the most beautiful church I have ever visited. I heard that people got upset that she spent so much on it, but she shut them down by saying that Jesus deserves the very best.

When folks get upset about making a church beautiful and say it's a waste of money, it makes me think of this passage from scripture:

> They gave a dinner for him there, and Martha served, while Lazarus was one of those reclining at table with him. Mary took a liter of costly perfumed oil made from genuine aromatic nard and anointed the feet of Jesus and dried them with her hair; the house was filled with the fragrance of the oil. Then Judas the Iscariot, one of his disciples, and the one who would betray him, said, "Why was this oil not sold for three hundred days' wages and given to the poor?" He said this not because he cared about the poor but because he was a thief and held the money bag and used to steal the contributions. So, Jesus said, "Leave her alone. Let her keep this for the day of my burial. You always have the poor with you, but you do not always have me." (John 12:2–8)

Now, I'm not saying that any person who complains about spending on making the church beautiful is a Judas. We've talked about the fact that we need to watch our spending so that St. Catherine's can effectively perform its mission. We just have to remember that investing our best efforts and resources in worship is always more important. The worship of God will always be the primary work of the Church.

DIRECTING OUR HEARTS AND MINDS TO GOD

A few weeks ago, you mentioned an idea that's been cooking in the back of your mind since you arrived. I don't know if you remember, but you were talking about replacing the old tabernacle with one that is more beautiful and designed to match the rest of the aesthetics of the Church.

I think it's a wonderful idea. The old tabernacle looks like it was designed in the 60's or 70's and seems out of place. You can ask around, but I don't think that anyone is particularly attached to it. It's too plain and abstract. The tabernacle should draw every person's eyes to it and direct their hearts to the supernatural reality that it's created to contain. It's nothing less than the Holy of Holies. The dwelling place of Jesus in the Most Blessed Sacrament! The beauty of the tabernacle should silently evangelize anyone who sees it.

I don't think expense is an obstacle. We just need to get a cost estimate for a new tabernacle and let people know that this is something you'd like to do. I guarantee that people will respond. You might even have someone step up with a $10,000 or $20,000 gift to cover the whole cost. Our parishioners WANT our church to be beautiful. They will be honored to provide a new tabernacle that is worthy of our Lord.

There's a great passage in the Old Testament that shares an inspiring story. God gives Moses a vision for the tabernacle that He wants to house the Ark of the Covenant. God describes in minute detail the materials needed and the plan of construction. Moses tells the people, and they respond with extraordinary generosity. In fact, at some point, Moses tells the Israelites to stop giving because they have more than enough (Exodus 36:4–7). Every fundraiser dreams of having that kind of problem.

MORE THAN A RESTORATION

You're called to do more at St. Catherine's than replace the furnace and put a new roof on the church. That is just maintenance. Your mission is to enhance it, to elevate it as a place of worship and house of prayer. When a visitor enters, they should be overwhelmed with the reality that they are stepping on holy ground. You don't run a community center; it's a Catholic Church! It doesn't need to be fancy or ornate. Some of the holiest places I've ever visited are very simple. But it must be reverent. Well fitted for its divine purpose.

Our church can be like an alabaster jar of perfumed oil poured on our Lord's feet by a grateful sinner. An outpouring of extravagant love made concrete. Of concrete. Using our gifts, our resources, to make that happen is a way of giving thanks to God for His great love for us.

Blessings,
The Almoner

P.S. If anyone does give you any push back on commissioning a new tabernacle, tell them to talk to Mrs. Sanderson. Our new food pantry can certainly use more supporters. It's not an either/or proposition between the new tabernacle and the food pantry. We can do ALL things through Christ who strengthens us.

39.

OUR BUCKET IS LEAKING!

Dear Fr. Zagloba,

I WAS TALKING TO Carmen about the church budget, and she mentioned that one of our big problems is that fewer and fewer people are responsible for filling our revenue budget. We got to looking at the numbers and saw that over the course of the past ten years the total number of parishioners has dropped by more than 20%.

You aren't surprised, are you? Father, you know the statistics about the decline in St. Catherine's membership, so I'm just pointing out the elephant in the room. Have you also noticed that the elephant is grey? The grey heads vastly outnumber the number of youths or young families. Are you concerned?

Now I don't want you to think that my main concern is whether we're going to reach the budget targets this year. The issue is much bigger than that. The budget is a symptom of a much larger problem. Kind of like discovering that my toddler has a fever but not knowing whether it's the flu or the bubonic plague. The budget issue points to a much bigger question.

THE PARABLE OF THE LEAKY BUCKET

There's an old parable that fundraisers use to talk about donors. Imagine a leaky bucket. You need to fill up a bucket, but it has holes. To make any headway, you need a scoop that adds water at least as fast as it runs out. You can fill some of the holes to slow the leaks, but the bucket isn't ever going to be watertight. How do you ever get that bucket full?

This analogy points to three very important fundraising concepts: donor attrition, donor retention, and donor acquisition.

The term "donor attrition" points to the reality that someone who donates today, who maybe has donated for a long time, may never donate again. The reality of donor attrition means that our donor base will eventually shrink to nothing if we do nothing to bring in new donors. Donor attrition is the leaks.

"Donor retention" is the concept that it takes fewer resources to keep a current donor than to find a new donor. By cultivating the organization's relationships with its donors, donor attrition is limited, and the withering of the donor file can be delayed or even reversed. Donor retention is plugging the holes.

One last concept, "donor acquisition." Donor acquisition is the strategies and programs that bring in new donors. Even with the best donor retention, donor attrition will eventually kill the organization if there isn't an intentional focus on donor acquisition. Donor acquisition is the scoop that pours more water into the bucket.

IS THE BUCKET HALF-EMPTY OR HALF-FULL?

Now think of our church as the bucket. Each of these fundraising concepts has their analogue in parish life. Our parish gets smaller when people stop attending. They move, pass away, or (God forbid) lose the faith. Compare this to donor attrition. When people get involved in the parish, when we feed them spiritually, they tend to stick around. Think of this as being like donor retention. When we invite and welcome new people to the Church, this is like donor acquisition.

Now I want to repeat; I don't want to focus on what the church is getting from these people. The budget is a side effect. We must focus on what they get from the Church. All people, every person who has ever been born, needs the saving love of Jesus Christ. If our church body isn't healthy and active, many people out there will never meet their Savior. There is no greater tragedy.

JUST HOW FIT IS THE BODY?

I want you to think about St. Catherine's incarnationally. Our parish is, quite literally, the mystical Body of Christ in miniature. How healthy do you think this Body is? St. Paul talks about each person being a member of the Body and possessing different gifts according to the part God created them to be. An eye and a hand are different, says the Apostle, and so there should be no bickering between them (1 Corinthians 12).

St. Paul was dealing with a different problem than we are. He had people who were contentious because the 'hand' thought itself more important than the 'eye.' We don't have this problem. Our problem is different. If you were to ask most of the people at St. Catherine's, they would tell you they have no idea if they are part of the hand, the eye, the toenail, or the appendix.

If you were to imagine the "Body" at St. Catherine's, would it look like a muscular Middle Eastern Carpenter, trained by a life of labor to carry the heaviest of Wood? Or is it more like a Modern American Couch Potato? In shape only to the extent that 'round' is technically a shape.

Or does it look like the parish demographics? Greying, slightly rheumatic, near-sighted, too tired to get up and do much of anything. "Oh, beauty ever ancient, ever new ..." I think we have a good handle on the ever-ancient part, but what about the ever new? Is the Body here at St. Catherine's constantly renewing itself the way it should? Or is it even suffering from leprosy, where pieces of the body (like our young people) are just falling away behind us as we totter around?

100 DAYS TO ROCK HARD ABS

I'm not suggesting that we need more activity simply for the sake of activity. Instead, try to imagine what this Body looks like when it is healthy and strong. "Time and Talent" at its very best means getting people engaged in the discovery of what part of the body God created them to be and supporting their activity so they can fulfill their purpose.

People who have the gift of evangelism need to be out evangelizing, the people who have the gift of administration should be organizing, the people who have the gift of hospitality should be welcoming people to the parish, etc. And when the Body is healthy, it will do what bodies do naturally. Grow. And since it is supernatural, it will grow until it reaches the full stature of Christ.

I don't think this will be easy or simple. If you've ever started working out after a long period of doing nothing, you know what your muscles normally do. They complain. They ache. They give out too soon. But gradually, through persistence, they become strong and supple. As the old Marine Corps saying goes, "pain is weakness leaving the body."

FILL THAT BUCKET WITH LIVING WATER

Jesus gave our church a mission: "Go therefore and make disciples. ..." It is St. Catherine's mission. Our mission is not, "Go, therefore, and make budget." If we focus on our central purpose, on what God created the Church to do, budgetary issues will take care of themselves.

If we as a parish focus on helping each person to discover their identity in Christ and learn how to live that to the fullest, our Church will overflow. Instead of worrying about dying of thirst, we'll have to start thinking about getting a bigger bucket.

Blessings,
The Almoner

40.

NOT A DRILL, A PLANNED EMERGENCY

Dear Fr. Zagloba,

TODAY I'M WRITING on a computer with a cracked screen. No idea how it happened, although two little boys are under investigation. It shouldn't be too expensive to fix, but it's inconvenient and supremely irritating.

Why do I bring this up? You've mentioned a couple of times that you are concerned about the air-conditioning unit at the Church. It has survived for decades, and it's starting to wheeze a little bit. I was surprised by the size of the quotes for replacing the units that you showed me. It makes sense, though, because they are custom built.

UNPLANNED AND PLANNED EMERGENCIES

There are two ways of dealing with the problem of aging infrastructure. One is the way I'm dealing with my computer screen. It wasn't a problem until it became a problem. Suddenly, it was a big problem. We'll call this the "unplanned emergency" approach. With my computer, it isn't such a big deal because it's only a couple hundred dollars. The air conditioners will cost over $100,000. That's nearly 20% of our annual budget. We're talking about an enormous problem.

I recommend the "planned emergency" approach, especially as a fundraiser. We know that this is going to be a problem at some point. If we start telling the parish about the need NOW, we can begin to gather the funds that we need before it becomes a crisis. This approach is a win-win. If the air-conditioning units last until we've raised all of the money, great! Run them until they die of old age. Or, do the repairs in the winter when it's convenient.

What if they break when we're only partway to our goal? Not ideal, but the crisis is considerably less severe because we would already have some of the money. Remember how much fun it was to raise the money on the fly when the furnace went up in smoke? You'll get to avoid some of that craziness because the campaign will already be moving. It's much easier to say, "We're already partway there, but now we need the rest of the money immediately," than "Yikes, we were unprepared and now we have to raise $100,000, so the Georgia heat doesn't melt us!"

I know the "planned emergency" approach works because I just applied it in my own life. You know my wife just had a baby. As soon as we learned that she was pregnant, I restructured our budget to put money away for the delivery. Of course, we had no idea that she would have to spend 11 days in the hospital, but we knew to expect substantial hospital bills. As a result, we're able to pay the bill with a minimum of trauma and financial stress. The plan worked!

TIMING IS EVERYTHING

We've almost completed raising the money to do the roof thanks to the matching funds that we got from Catholic Extension Society. I think that we'll be pretty much wrapped up by the time the new year rolls around. You just need to mention how close we are to the goal over the next couple weeks. Keep it fresh in everyone's minds.

Once we hit that target, we should immediately pull the trigger on installing the new roof. Everyone in the parish will get the gratifying feeling of seeing their donations go to work. Once the roofers finish the job, we should wait a month or so before announcing the new air-conditioning campaign. We will have several months before the Bishop's annual appeal starts so we can get some momentum going before everyone gets distracted.

I think that we should approach this campaign in a similar way to the roof campaign. Right now, it's not an EMERGENCY, so we don't have to be super intense about it. Mention it during the announcements regularly. A progress display in the narthex. I don't think we'll be eligible for another matching grant for a while, but it's worth asking to find out if we can do one in 6 months or a year. I also think that you should incorporate the direct personal requests that worked so well when the furnace blew up.

I don't think that it's a huge problem that we're transitioning from one fundraising campaign to another. People who research fundraising have learned that donors who have recently given are the most likely to give again. They have already demonstrated their willingness to give. You just have to ask again.

THE PURGATORY OF PERPETUAL FUNDRAISING

Now I do have to admit; it's kind of terrible to be in perpetual fundraising mode. I think we don't have any pressing repair needs once we replace the air-conditioning unit. After we finish this campaign, we should probably take a rest from campaign mode. Give everyone's wallets a chance to rest.

In the long-term, we should be investing our energy in developing into a stewardship parish. If even 30% of our parishioners were living stewardship and tithing a full 10%, your biggest responsibility would be trying to discern how to spend the surplus.

Blessings,
The Almoner

41.

ENDOWMENTS—TENDING THE ORCHARD

Dear Fr. Zagloba,

I'VE GOT EXCITING NEWS. I just emailed the final documents to Jim at the Catholic Foundation. St. Catherine's now officially has an endowment. That's one small step for a fundraiser and one giant leap for St. Catherine's.

Now we need to figure out a way to tell people about it. Raising money for an endowment is a marathon, not a sprint. It would be a wonderful surprise if we got some big gifts right off the bat, but we probably won't start getting gifts in any significant number for 5–7 years.

When we first started talking about creating an endowment, I compared it with planting an apple seed. This analogy is very useful here. Now that we have planted the seed, we will tend the orchard for the next several years without seeing any fruit. We will need to invest in this orchard—time, energy, resources—if we ever want the satisfaction of biting into that first piece of crisp, delicious fruit.

BUILD A DRIP WATERING SYSTEM

With a long-term effort like this, it's important to have a marketing plan that will slowly but consistently make people aware of the endowment's existence. I suggest that we combine four different elements to make our "watering system."

Regular announcements—It's hard to beat you standing up at the end of Mass and telling folks about the endowment and inviting them to consider writing a gift to the endowment in their will. Not all the time, mind you, but it needs to part of the annual calendar of announcements. You should at least mention it in the fall when we're doing our annual stewardship renewal and in the spring when you kick off the Bishop's annual appeal.

Bulletin advertising—People take their bulletins home. They certainly at least thumb through it, because otherwise, they would leave them on the back table. What we put into the bulletin doesn't have to be huge and wordy. It doesn't have to change all the time. All it needs is the name of the endowment, a phrase like "Please consider leaving a legacy by making a gift to St. Catherine's endowment. For more information call …"

Website information—We can add a section to the website with information about ways to give to the endowment. We don't want to overwhelm people with information, but we should at least mention the following ways to give to the endowment: bequests, gifts of stock, insurance policies, gifts of real estate, and retirement accounts.

Legacy Society—One big way to encourage people to let us know to expect a gift is to start a legacy society. Once a parishioner notifies us of an intended gift, the legacy society makes sure they feel thanked and appreciated. We can host an annual legacy society dinner catered by the Church to say thank you. Eventually, we'll want to set up a 'Legacy Wall' which thanks all the donors that have made either gifts or gift commitments. We can honor the new members of the legacy society at each annual dinner. You can mention it when you're announcing the endowment and we can also create a brochure promoting the legacy society for the brochure rack in the Narthex.

These four elements should let most people know that the endowment exists and encourage them to give. If we had more money, we could pay a staff person to go out and personally asked people to make gifts from their estates to the endowment. In fundraising terms, this person would be called a "Planned Giving Officer." We don't have that kind of money. I only mention it so you know we could do more with more resources.

SELECTING THE FERTILIZER

I think the "why" of promoting the endowment is even more important than the "how." It's the fertilizer that will keep it growing. Planned giving and estate gifts are typically the biggest gifts that people ever make in their lives. A planned gift might be anywhere from 10–100 times larger than any gift they have ever made to anything. Focusing on the "why" is especially important.

Since we're in the Advent season, we have a feast day that provides us a deeper understanding of what giving to the Church is all about. I know your thoughts immediately go to Christmas, which is the most giving-est holiday of the year, but that's not what should pull our focus. No, I'm thinking of Epiphany, the feast of the Three Kings.

Remember what the kings told Herod? They wanted to find the new King, so they might worship him. When they found Jesus, they worshipped him and brought him gifts. It seems obvious to me that bringing gifts is a part of their worship. They didn't just bring any gifts; they brought gifts fit for a king. Gold, frankincense, and myrrh.

A gift to the endowment should be an act of worship for the donor. A gift at the end of their life to give thanks to God for all that He has so generously given to them. It should be the best gift they have ever given, and they should be encouraged to give joyfully because they know that such a gift will help to support the work of the Church for generations to come.

TEND THE ORCHARD

With the right fertilizer and the right irrigation system, our endowment will start producing fruit. If we continue to tend our little "orchard," it will continue to grow—both through new gifts and sound investment strategy. It will take years before it becomes what we envision it to be. In fact, you will probably be off in another parish before it begins to produce income that will transform St. Catherine's. But YOUR legacy and the endowment that you started will go on and on.

Blessings
The Almoner

42.

A CHRISTMAS FAREWELL

Dear Fr. Zagloba,

SOMETHING UNEXPECTED has happened. We're moving. My wife and I have wanted to move out to the country for years now, and the house right next to her parents has come up for sale. Unbeatable price, perfect location. The lot that falls to me is my delight.

Unfortunately, this means we're going to be moving to a new parish and a different diocese. I say new, but it's the church where my wife was baptized. New for me. It will be a good change, but it means that I'm going to have to resign from the Pastoral Council. Things are moving quickly, and we're hoping to move during my Christmas vacation. It has been a bit of a whirlwind, but here are a few parting thoughts.

KEEP THE RIGHT FOCUS

One of the things that I've learned in helping you raise money for St. Catherine's is that the devil wants to keep us focused on the "how," specifically on "how on earth are we going to raise the $????????? to do (fill in the blank)?" It's a question that can torment us until we are completely paralyzed and can't accomplish anything. God, on the other hand, wants us to remember His instruction, "Seek ye first the kingdom of God and all these things will be added unto you." If we're focused on understanding WHAT He wants us to do and WHY He wants us to do it, He'll give us the resources we need to make it happen. As an old Southern fundraiser once told me, "If it's God's will, it's God's bill."

As you're seeking God's will for St. Catherine's, don't be afraid to be bold. God calls the saints to be audacious in His service. He calls them to do impossible things. That little corner of the city needs the Gospel. You're responsible for getting the Word out. Don't let the devil scare you with the "how." Instead, stay focused on why God put you here and what His plan is for your little flock.

When you do get to the question of "how?" remember that failure is not an option. It's mandatory. You will try fundraising strategies that will flop terribly. You won't get the response you expected; you won't get the volunteers you needed, you will feel like you're trying to build a pyramid by yourself with a rusty hammer. Welcome to the cross of fundraising. It's good for you … Miracle Grow for the virtue of humility. Get up and try again. Seek God's will and the ways He wants you to raise the money for His plans to come to fruition. Test new fundraising strategies and hold onto those that work. Discard those that don't.

ASK, ASK, ASK, ASK, ASK

Jesus said, "Ask, and you shall receive." You can also read that and understand, "Don't ask, and you won't receive." I've heard too many times from people that they would like to raise money like George Muller, the English Protestant who told God that he would start an orphanage if he never had to raise any money for it. Mind you, he never asked anyone (besides God) for money, and was given enough funds to serve thousands of children for decades.

Yes, God can inspire people to give directly. It's true. But asking for money is not evil. It's an opportunity. It's a ministry. It's a way to invite people into the mission. There are a lot of people out there who don't have the flexibility to be a missionary on another continent. But they're more than happy to be a part of the mission by providing the resources needed to put the missionaries on a plane. Or build a school. Or a cathedral, for that matter. You're giving them the opportunity to do something good that they could never do alone.

When we think about Jesus's disciples, our minds automatically go to "the Twelve." But they were not alone in following and serving Jesus. There were others behind the scenes. During his ministry, Jesus was supported financially and materially by Joanna and Susanna, as well as others. Since He is God, He could have created everything He needed out of nothing, but instead, He chose to invite some to participate in His mission through their generosity. These women helped him to build His kingdom just as surely as His apostles did but in a different way. God meets us where we are and invites us to use the gifts He has given us to accomplish His purposes.

MISSION FROM GOD

"You were not made for comfort. You were made for greatness." This quote from Pope Benedict XVI should stir your blood. I love it. The call of the Gospel is not about teaching everybody to be nice and live out our lives with a minimum of unpleasantness. It's a ringing challenge to become a saint and shake the pillars of creation.

Remember the mission. "Go therefore and make disciples. ..." At St. Catherine's, you are the disciple-maker. You're the one that calls people out of their safe little boxes, trains them, and then sends them out on mission. No one can replace you. You're ordained by God to do it. I know it's sometimes hard to think of your parishioners as disciples, but just look at what Mrs. Sanderson and Mr. Jenson have done in putting together the food pantry. Every month, new people are being touched by the Church and by the Gospel because you said, "Yes" to a little old lady who wanted to feed the poor.

You'll have to knock on a lot of doors. There are people in the parish who have talents that they should be putting at the service of the Gospel, but they need you to invite them into the mission. Until they begin their divine mission, they are only living a shadow of a life. You might have to shake them out of their comfort and give them a taste of the greatness that God has in store for them.

I bet many will surprise you. I never would have thought that Mrs. Sanderson was the anointed one for starting our ministry to the poor, or that she would be able to convince Mr. Jenson to help her. Now they're rolling along, and they're getting more and more people involved. Every disciple that you make will begin to multiply. Disciples make more disciples.

BLESSINGS!

Now, it's not like I'm disappearing into the African Congo. I still work in town and will be happy to brainstorm fundraising ideas with you over tacos. I've enjoyed helping you raise money for St. Catherine's more than I can tell you.

Besides, I think you're ready to fly on your own. You've started stewardship, online giving, major gifts, and an endowment. You have parishioners who have learned how to do mission fundraising. You still enjoy the brownies from the bake sales, but you know there's an easier way to fix the roof than spending the next two years in the kitchen.

May the Lord bless you, inspire you, and encourage you in your ministry. May He multiply your flock. And thank you for allowing me to serve.

Blessings,
The Almoner

Index

aging infrastructure, 173
alms, 56, 149
annual stewardship campaign, 91, 97
begging, 9
Body of Christ, 171
budget, 169
capital campaign, 29, 75
Catholic Extension Society, 75, 135
Catholic foundation, 177
Catholic Stewardship Consultants, 61
charitable enterprise, 5
charity, 105
Code of Canon Law, 138
committees, 32
community relations, 118
Compass Catholic Ministries, 128, 159, 161
diaconate, 27
discipleship, 97, 115
donor acquisition, 132, 170
donor attrition, 170
donor retention, 170
endowment, 83, 177
engagement, 145
entitlement, 105
face-to-face fundraising, 79

faithfulness, 157
food pantry, 67, 79, 151
food stamps, 105, 107
fundraising, 2, 55
fundraising strategies, 182
grant, 75, 135
Grateful and Giving, by Deacon Don McArdle, 61
impulse charity, 87, 113
in-kind donation, 117
Johann Tetzel, 22
justice, 156
Lazarus, 55
legacy society, 178
major gift fundraising, 43
major gifts, 43, 47, 51
Mammon, 137
matching gift, 75
mercy, 55, 149, 157
ministry support fundraising, 68
mission team, 114
mission trips, 114
Msgr. Thomas McGread, 61
offertory, 13, 17
online giving, 71, 81
person-to-person fundraising, 102
planned emergency, 173
planned giving, 178

planning, 28
prosperity gospel, 121
raise money, 1, 181
requests for support, 117
Salvation Army, 89
second collection, 113
Simon Magus, 21
simony, 21
social justice, 58
St. Matthew, 17
steward, 37
stewardship, 2, 115, 127, 155, 161
Stewardship
   a Disciple's Response, 61, 97, 138

stewardship campaign, 21, 37
stock gifts, 135
talents, 92, 98
thank you, 52, 151
time, talent, and treasure, 91
tithe, 91, 93, 137
vision, 31
volunteer, 32
volunteer fundraisers, 101
volunteer solicitation, 109
volunteers, 102
website, 71, 145, 178
worship, 165

www.ingramcontent.com/pod-product-compliance
Lightning Source LLC
Chambersburg PA
CBHW020411080526
44584CB00014B/1283